The Super-Fast
Anti-Inflammatory Recipe Book

Easy and Fast Recipes for a Balanced Lifestyle

Thomas Jollif

o

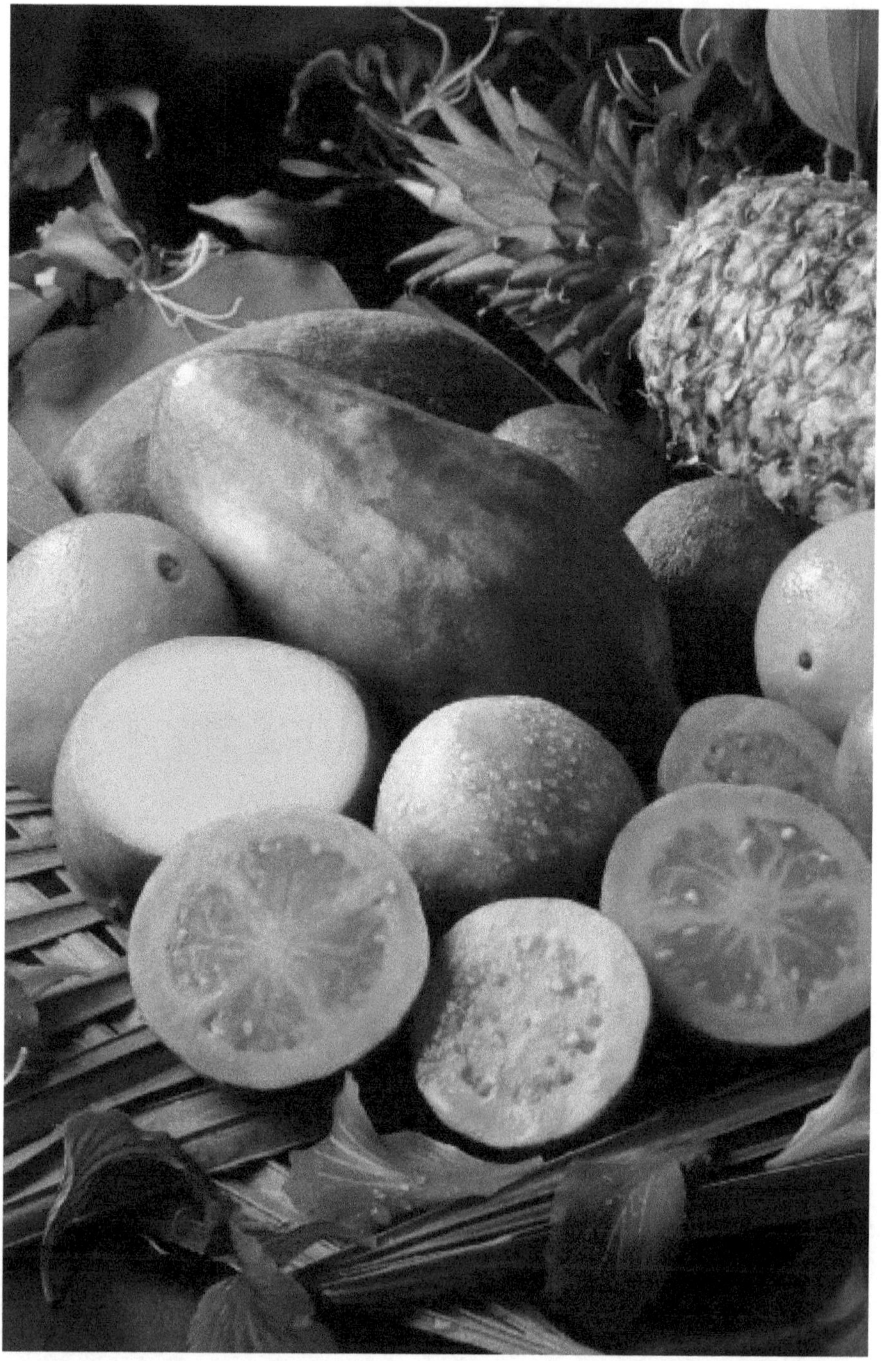

by reading this document, the reader agrees that under no circumstances is the author responsible for any losses, direct or indirect, which are incurred as a result of the use of information contained within this document, including, but not limited to, — errors, omissions, or inaccuracies.

Table of Contents

BREAKFASTS 7

BANANA CASHEW TOAST.. 7

BANANA PANCAKES.. 9

BANANA-OATMEAL VEGAN PANCAKES........................11

BARLEY BREAKFAST BOWL WITH LEMON YOGURT SAUCE.......... 13

BEEF BREAKFAST CASSEROLE.......................................15

BLUEBERRY & CASHEW WAFFLES....................................17

BLUEBERRY-BRAN BREAKFAST SUNDAE 19

BREAKFAST ARROZCALDO 21

BREAKFAST PITAS 23

BREAKFAST SAUSAGE AND MUSHROOM CASSEROLE 25

SMOOTHIES AND DRINKS 28

BLACKBERRY ITALIAN DRINK 28

BLENDED COCONUT MILK AND BANANA BREAKFAST SMOOTHIE 30

BLUEBERRY AND SPINACH SHAKE 32

BLUEBERRY LIME JUICE 34

BLUEBERRY MATCHA SMOOTHIE...................................36

BLUEBERRY POMEGRANATE SMOOTHIE 38

BLUEBERRY SMOOTHIE 39

SIDES 40

CITRUS COUSCOUS WITH HERB *40*

COOL GARBANZO AND SPINACH BEANS *42*

COUSCOUS SALAD *43*

CREAMY POLENTA *45*

CRISPY CORN *47*

SAUCES AND DRESSINGS **49**

BEAN POTATO SPREAD *49*

CASHEW GINGER DIP *51*

SNACKS **53**

AVOCADO HUMMUS *53*

AVOCADO WITH TOMATOES AND CUCUMBER *55*

BAKED VEGGIE TURMERIC NUGGETS *57*

BERRY DELIGHT *59*

BERRY ENERGY BITES *61*

BLUEBERRY & CHIA FLAX SEED PUDDING *62*

BOILED OKRA AND SQUASH *64*

SOUPS AND STEWS **66**

CARROT BROCCOLI STEW *66*

CARROT, GINGER & TURMERIC SOUP *68*

CAULIFLOWER AND CLAM CHOWDER *70*

CAULIFLOWER, COCONUT MILK, AND SHRIMP SOUP *72*

CELERY SOUP *74*

CHEESY BROCCOLI SOUP *76*

CHEESY CHICKEN SOUP *78*

CHEESY TOMATO AND BASIL SOUP 80

CHICKEN AND CAULIFLOWER CURRY STEW 83

CHICKEN AND KALE SOUP...85

DESSERTS 87

BANANA CINNAMON 87

BANANA CINNAMON COOKIES 89

BEET PANCAKES 91

BERRY ICE POPS 93

BERRY PARFAIT 95

BERRY-BANANA YOGURT 97

BLACK TEA CAKE 99

BLUEBERRY CRISP 101

BLUEBERRY ENERGY BITES 103

BLUEBERRY SOUR CREAM CAKE 105

BREAKFASTS

Banana Cashew Toast

Time To Prepare: ten minutes

Time to Cook: 0 minutes

Yield: Servings 3

Ingredients:

- 1 cup roasted cashews (unsalted)
- 2 ripe moderate-sized bananas
- 2 tsp. flax meals
- 2 tsp. honey
- 4 pieces oat bread
- Dash of salt
- Pinch of cinnamon

Directions:

1. Peel and slice the bananas into ½-inch pieces. Toast the bread. Use a food processor to puree the salt and cashews until they are smooth. Use the puree as a spread on the toasts. On top of the spread, position a layer of bananas.
2. Put in flax meals and a dash of cinnamon on top of the bananas. Top the toast with honey.

Nutritional Info: Calories: 634 kcal ‖ Protein: 13.42 g ‖ Fat: 47.6 g ‖ Carbohydrates: 48.02

Banana Pancakes

Time To Prepare: five minutes

Time to Cook: fifteen minutes

Yield: Servings 2

Ingredients:

- ½ Teaspoon Sea Salt
- 1 Banana, Ripe
- 1 Cup Rolled Oats
- 1 Egg White
- 1 Tablespoon Coconut Oil, Divided
- 1 Teaspoon Vanilla Extract, Pure
- 2 Eggs
- 2 Teaspoons Ground Cinnamon

Directions:

1. Prepare your food processor, grinding your oats until they make a coarse flour.

2. Put in your cinnamon, egg whites, eggs, banana, vanilla, and salt. Blend until it becomes a smooth batter, and then heat a small frying pan on moderate heat. Heat a half a tablespoon of coconut oil, and then pour your batter in. Cook for a couple of minutes per side, and carry on till all of your batter has been used.

Nutritional Info: Calories: 306 ǁ Protein: fifteen Grams ǁ Fat: fifteen Grams ǁ Carbohydrates: 17 Grams

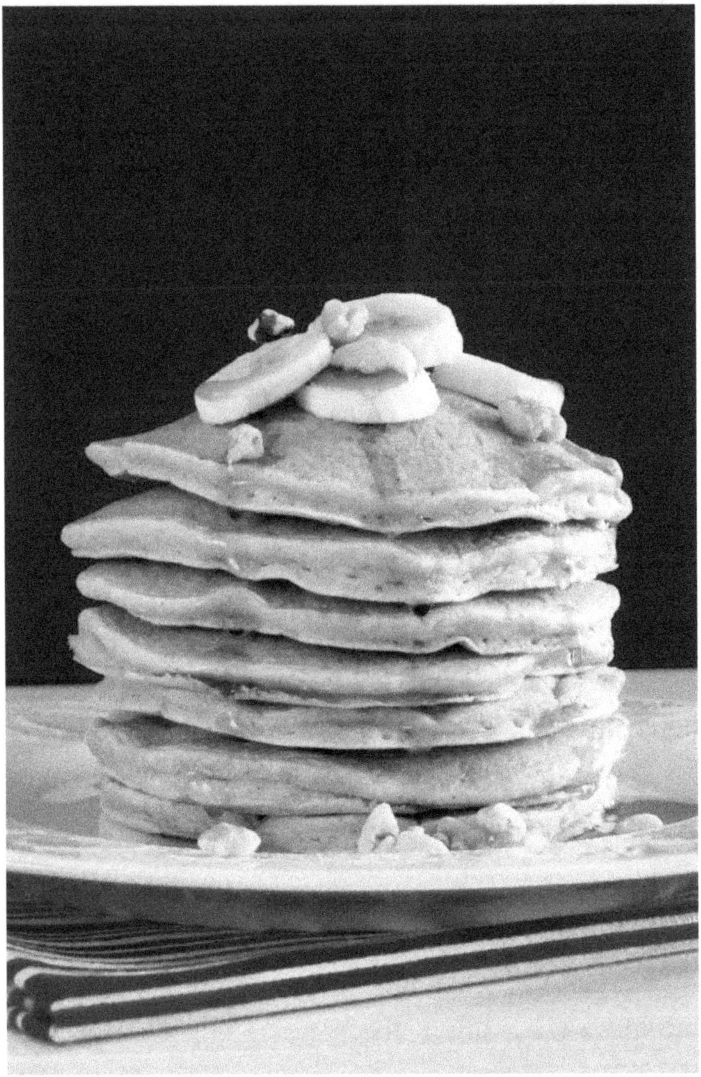

Banana-Oatmeal Vegan Pancakes

Time To Prepare: five minutes
Time to Cook: five minutes
Yield: Servings 12

Ingredients:

- ½ c. organic whole wheat flour
- ½ tsp. sea salt
- 1¼ c. old fashioned oats
- 1½ c. soymilk
- 2 ripe bananas
- 2 tsp. Baking powder

Directions:

1. To begin, heat griddle or frying pan on moderate heat.
2. After this, place all ingredients, apart from for banana, into a blender and process until the desired smoothness is achieved. Put in the bananas to blender and blend until the desired smoothness is achieved.
3. Lightly grease griddle with olive or coconut oil, then pour ¼ c. of batter onto griddle and cook for minimum two to three minutes, then flip and cook for approximately 2 minutes or maximum the pancake is golden brown and thoroughly cooked.
4. Repeat process with remaining batter.

Nutritional Info: Calories: 59 kcal ‖ Protein: 3.49 g ‖ Fat: 1.48 g ‖ Carbohydrates: 11.52 g

Barley Breakfast Bowl with Lemon Yogurt Sauce

Time To Prepare: ten minutes

Time to Cook: 0 minutes

Yield: Servings 2

Ingredients:

- ¼ c. cut almonds, toasted
- ¼ c. fresh mint or parsley, chopped
- ¼ tsp. fresh ground black pepper
- ¼ tsp. kosher salt
- ½ tsp. Sea salt
- 1 c. Greek plain yogurt
- 1 c. mung bean sprouts (or preferred variety)
- 1 small avocado – peeled/pitted, and flesh diced or cut
- 1 tsp. Fresh lemon juice
- 1 tsp. lemon zest, finely grated
- 1/3 c. Cotija cheese or queso fresco - crumbled
- 1½ c. cooked barley, keep warm
- Fresh ground black pepper, to taste
- Lemon Yogurt Sauce
- Sea salt, to taste

Directions:

1. First, prepare the Lemon Yogurt Sauce: Mix the plain yogurt, lemon zest and juice, fresh mint or parsley, and salt

& pepper in a container and stir to combine well. Cover and place in your fridge until ready to serve.

2. After this, prepare the barley container: In a small mixing container, mix the barley, bean sprouts, cheese, almonds, and salt. Stir to mix thoroughly.

3. Split barley mixture into 2 serving bowls. Top each barley container with 2 tbsp. lemon yogurt sauce and avocado. Place a pinch of salt and pepper to taste, serve, and enjoy!

Nutritional Info: Calories: 432 kcal ‖ Protein: 13.6 g ‖ Fat: 23.37 g ‖ Carbohydrates: 47.62 g

Beef Breakfast Casserole

Time To Prepare: ten minutes

Time to Cook: thirty minutes

Yield: Servings 5

Ingredients:

- ¼ cup cut black olives
- ½ cup Pico de Gallo
- 1 cup baby spinach
- 1 pound of ground beef, cooked
- 10 eggs
- Freshly ground black pepper

Directions:

1. Preheat your oven to 350 degrees Fahrenheit. Prepare a 9" glass pie plate with non-stick spray.
2. Whisk the eggs until frothy. Sprinkle with salt and pepper.
3. Layer the cooked ground beef, Pico de Gallo, and spinach in the pie plate.
4. Slowly pour the eggs over the top.
5. Top with black olives.
6. Bake for minimum 30 minutes, until firm in the center.
7. Cut into 5 pieces before you serve.

Nutritional Info: Calories: 479 kcal ‖ Protein: 43.54 g ‖ Fat: 30.59 g ‖ Carbohydrates: 4.65 g

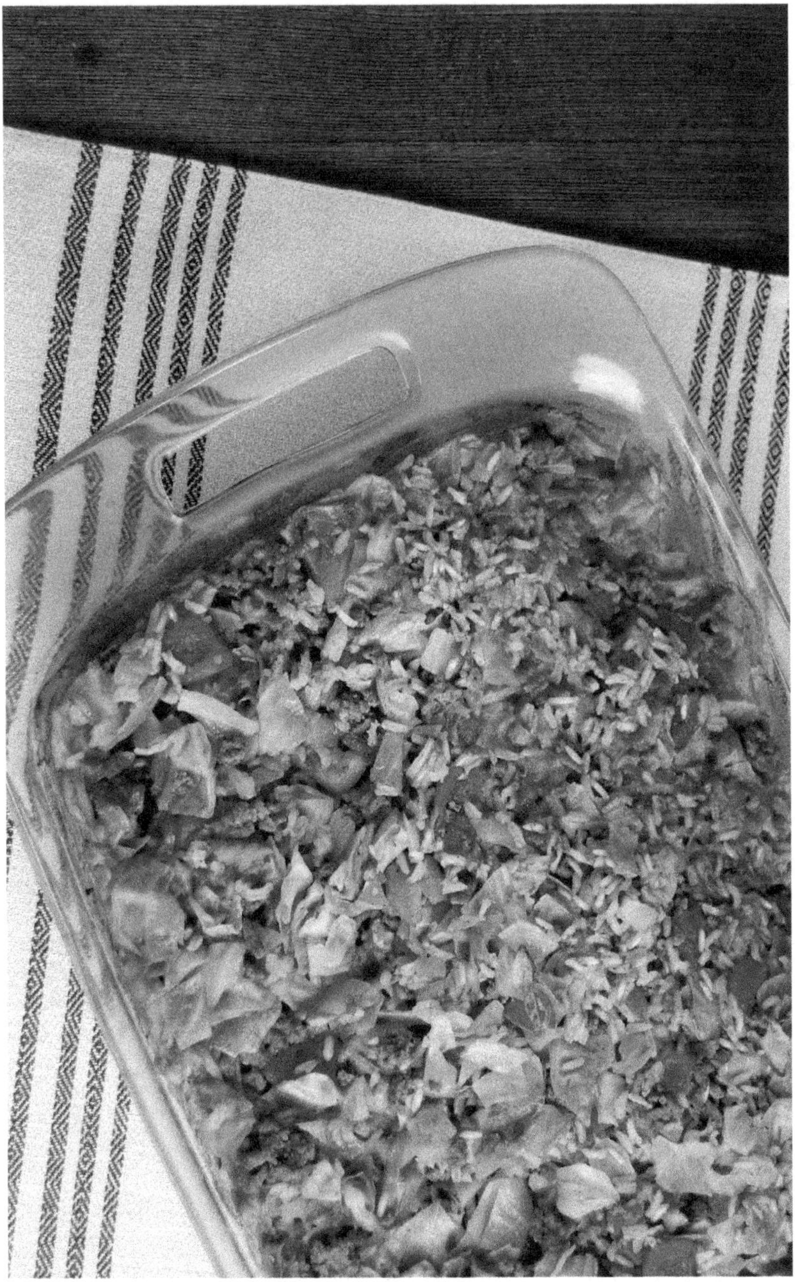

Blueberry & Cashew Waffles

Time To Prepare: fifteen minutes

Time to Cook: 4-5 minutes

Yield: Servings 5

Ingredients:

- ¼ cup coconut oil, melted
- ½ cup unsweetened almond milk
- ½ teaspoon organic vanilla flavor
- 1 cup fresh blueberries
- 1 cup raw cashews
- 1 tsp baking soda
- 3 organic eggs
- 3 tablespoons coconut flour
- 3 tablespoons organic honey
- Salt, to taste

Directions:

1. Preheat the waffle iron after which grease it.
2. In a mixer, put in cashews and pulse till flour-like consistency forms.
3. Move the cashew flour in a big container.
4. Put in almond flour, baking soda and salt and mix thoroughly.

5. In another container, put the rest of the ingredients and beat till well blended.
6. Place the egg mixture into the flour mixture then mix till well blended.
7. Fold in blueberries.
8. In preheated waffle iron, put in the required amount of mixture.
9. Cook for about five minutes.
10. Repeat with the rest of the mixture.

Nutritional Info: Calories: 432 ‖ Fat: 32 ‖ Carbohydrates: 32g ‖ Protein: 13g

Blueberry-Bran Breakfast Sundae

Time To Prepare: ten minutes
Time to Cook: 0 minutes
Yield: Servings 2

Ingredients:

- 1/4 c. fresh blueberries
- 2 c. bran flakes
- 2 c. vanilla or lemon-flavored low-fat yogurt (if possible Greek yogurt) or flavor of choice.
- 2 tbsp. chopped pecans (or nuts of choice)
- 2 tbsp. cut almonds (or nuts of choice)
- 2 tbsp. dried cranberries (or dried or fresh fruit of choice)

Directions:

1. In a container, place 1 c. yogurt, and one c. bran flakes.
2. Top with 1/8 c. fresh blueberries, followed by 1 tbsp. Each of cut almonds, chopped pecans, and dried cranberries.
3. Repeat using the rest of the ingredients to make a second serving. Serve instantly.

Nutritional Info: Calories: 420 kcal ‖ Protein: 21.12 g ‖ Fat: 13.58 g ‖ Carbohydrates: 59.8 g

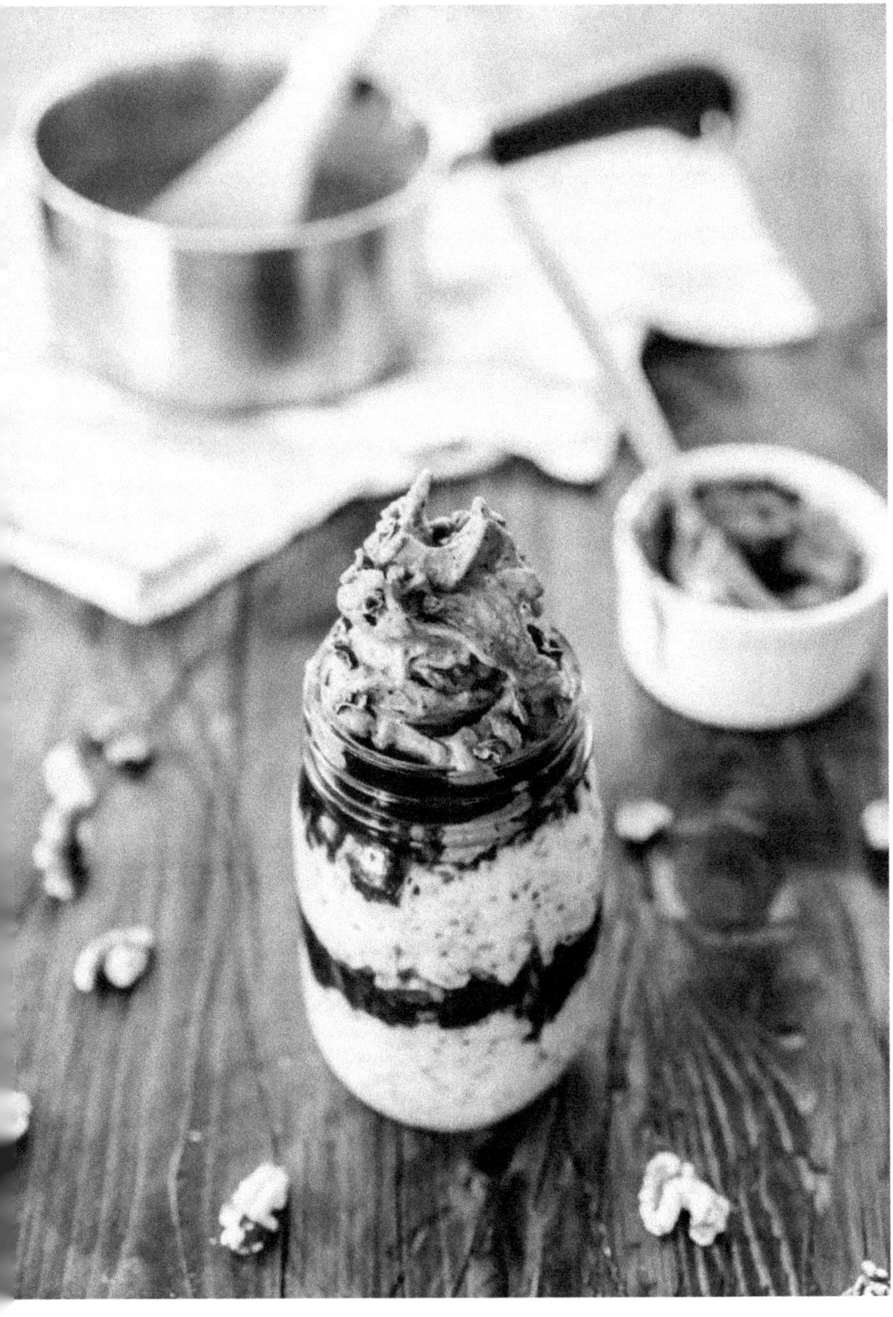

Breakfast Arrozcaldo

Time To Prepare: twenty minutes
Time to Cook: thirty minutes
Yield: Servings 5

Ingredients:

- ¼ cup raisins
- ½ cup frozen peas, thawed
- 1 garlic clove, minced
- 1 white onion, minced
- 1½ cups brown rice, cooked
- 6 eggs, white only
- For the filling
- oil, for greasing

Directions:

1. To make the filling, spray a small amount of oil into a frying pan set on moderate heat. Put in in onion and garlic. Stir-fry until former is limp and transparent.
2. Stir-fry while breaking up clumps, approximately 2 minutes. Put in in rest of the ingredients. Stir-fry for one more minute.
3. Turn down the heat, and let filling cook for ten to fifteen minutes, or until juices are greatly reduced. Stir frequently. Turn off heat. Split into 6 equivalent portions.

4. For the eggs, spray a small amount of oil into a smaller frying pan set on moderate heat. Cook eggs. Discard yolk. Move to holding the plate.

5. To serve, place 1 portion of rice on a plate, 1 portion of filling, and 1 egg white. Serve warm.

Nutritional Info: Calories: 53 kcal ‖ Protein: 6.28 g ‖ Fat: 1.35 g ‖ Carbohydrates: 3.59 g

Breakfast Pitas

Time To Prepare: 4 minutes
Time to Cook: six minutes
Yield: Servings 4

Ingredients:

- 1 c. raw spinach (cook if you prefer)
- 1 tsp. garlic powder
- 1 tsp. onion powder
- 2 c. bell peppers, chopped (any color)
- 2 tsp. extra virgin olive oil
- 4 whole-wheat pita pockets
- 8 egg whites

Directions:

1. Place the olive oil to a big sauté pan and place on moderate heat. When the oil is hot in shiny, throw in the bell pepper and sauté for approximately 3 minutes or until soft. Put in in the spinach now (if you wish it cooked) and sauté for approximately 1 to three minutes or just up to the sides begins to wilt.

2. Put the egg whites into a small container, whisk well. Put in in spices; whisk well. Pour the egg mixture into the sauté pan and scramble everything together.

3. Turn off the heat and stuff ½ to 1 c. mixture into a pita pocket before you serve.

23

Nutritional Info: Calories: 153 kcal ‖ Protein: 12.4 g ‖ Fat: 3.41 g ‖ Carbohydrates: 19.32 g

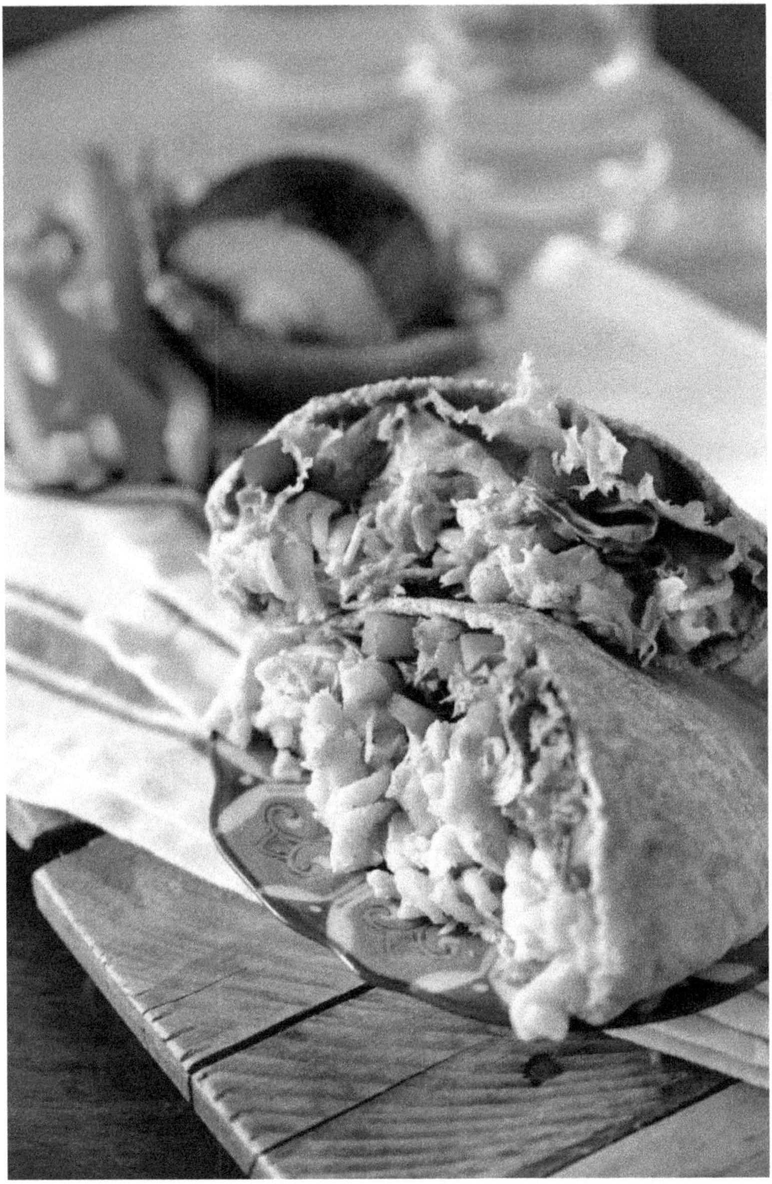

Breakfast Sausage and Mushroom Casserole

Time To Prepare: twenty minutes

Time to Cook: forty-five minutes

Yield: Servings 4

Ingredients:

- 1 ½ tsp. of sea salt, divided
- 1 medium onion, finely diced
- 1 red bell pepper, roasted
- 2 Tablespoons of organic ghee
- 3/4 tsp. of ground black pepper, divided
- 450g of Italian sausage, cooked and crumbled
- 6 free-range eggs
- 600g of sweet potatoes
- 8 ounces of white mushrooms, cut
- Three-fourth cup of coconut milk

Directions:

1. Peel and shred the sweet potatoes.
2. Take a container, fill it with ice-cold water, and soak the sweet potatoes in it. Set aside.
3. Peel the roasted bell pepper, remove its seeds and finely dice it.
4. Set the oven 375°F.

5. Get a casserole baking dish and grease it with the organic ghee.

6. Place a frying pan using moderate heat and cook the mushrooms in it. Cook until the mushrooms are crunchy and brown.

7. Take the mushrooms out and mix them with the crumbled sausage.

8. Now sauté the onions in the same frying pan. Cook up to the onions are tender and golden. This should take approximately four – five minutes.

9. Take the onions out and mix them in the sausage-mushroom mixture.

10. Put in the diced bell pepper to the same mixture.

11. Mix thoroughly and set aside for a while.

12. Now drain the soaked shredded potatoes, put them on a paper towel, and pat dry.

13. Bring the sweet potatoes in a container and put in about a teaspoon of salt and half a teaspoon of ground black pepper to it. Mix thoroughly and save for later.

14. Now take a big container and crack the eggs in it.

15. Break the eggs and then mix in the coconut milk.

16. Mix in the rest of the black pepper and salt.

17. Take the greased casserole dish and spread the seasoned sweet potatoes uniformly in the base of the dish.

18. After this, spread the sausage mixture uniformly in the dish.

19. To finish, spread the egg mixture.

20. Now cover the casserole dish using a piece of aluminium foil.

21. Bake for 20 - thirty minutes. To check if the casserole is baked properly, insert a tester in the center of the casserole, and it should come out clean.

22. Uncover the casserole dish and bake it again, uncovered for 5 - ten minutes, until the casserole is a little golden on the top.

23. Let it cool for approximately ten minutes.

24. Enjoy!

Nutritional Info: Calories: 598 kcal ‖ Protein: 28.65 g ‖ Fat: 36.75 g ‖ Carbohydrates: 48.01 g

SMOOTHIES AND DRINKS

Blackberry Italian Drink

Time To Prepare: five minutes

Time to Cook: fifteen minutes

Yield: Servings 4

Ingredients:

- 1 bottle sparkling water
- 1 cup blackberries
- 1 lemon, cut
- 2 tbsp. honey

Directions:

1. Put in 1 cup (non-carbonated) water to the instant pot.
2. Put in blackberries to the instant pot.
3. Secure the lid. Cook on HIGH pressure ten minutes.
4. When done, depressurize naturally.
5. Mash the berries in the instant pot. Move to dish. Let cool.
6. As blackberries cook, in a separate small deep cooking pan with a heavy bottom. Put in honey. Simmer five minutes. Cool down.
7. To make the drink. Ladle 1 teaspoon honey. Pour in fruit mixture. Put in carbonated water. Stir.

Nutritional Info: Calories: 249 ‖ Fat: 0.6g ‖ Carbohydrates: 55g ‖ Protein: 7.5g

Blended Coconut Milk and Banana Breakfast Smoothie

Time To Prepare: ten minutes

Time to Cook: 0 minutes

Yield: Servings 4

Ingredients:

- 2 cups almond milk
- 2 cups coconut milk
- 4 ripe moderate-sized bananas
- 4 tbsp. flax seeds
- 4 tsp. cinnamon

Directions:

1. Peel the banana and cut it into ½-inch pieces. Put all the ingredients in the blender and blend into a smoothie.
2. Put in a dash of cinnamon at the top of the smoothie before you serve.

Nutritional Info: Calories: 332 kcal ‖ Protein: 12.49 g ‖ Fat: 14.42 g ‖ Carbohydrates: 42.46 g

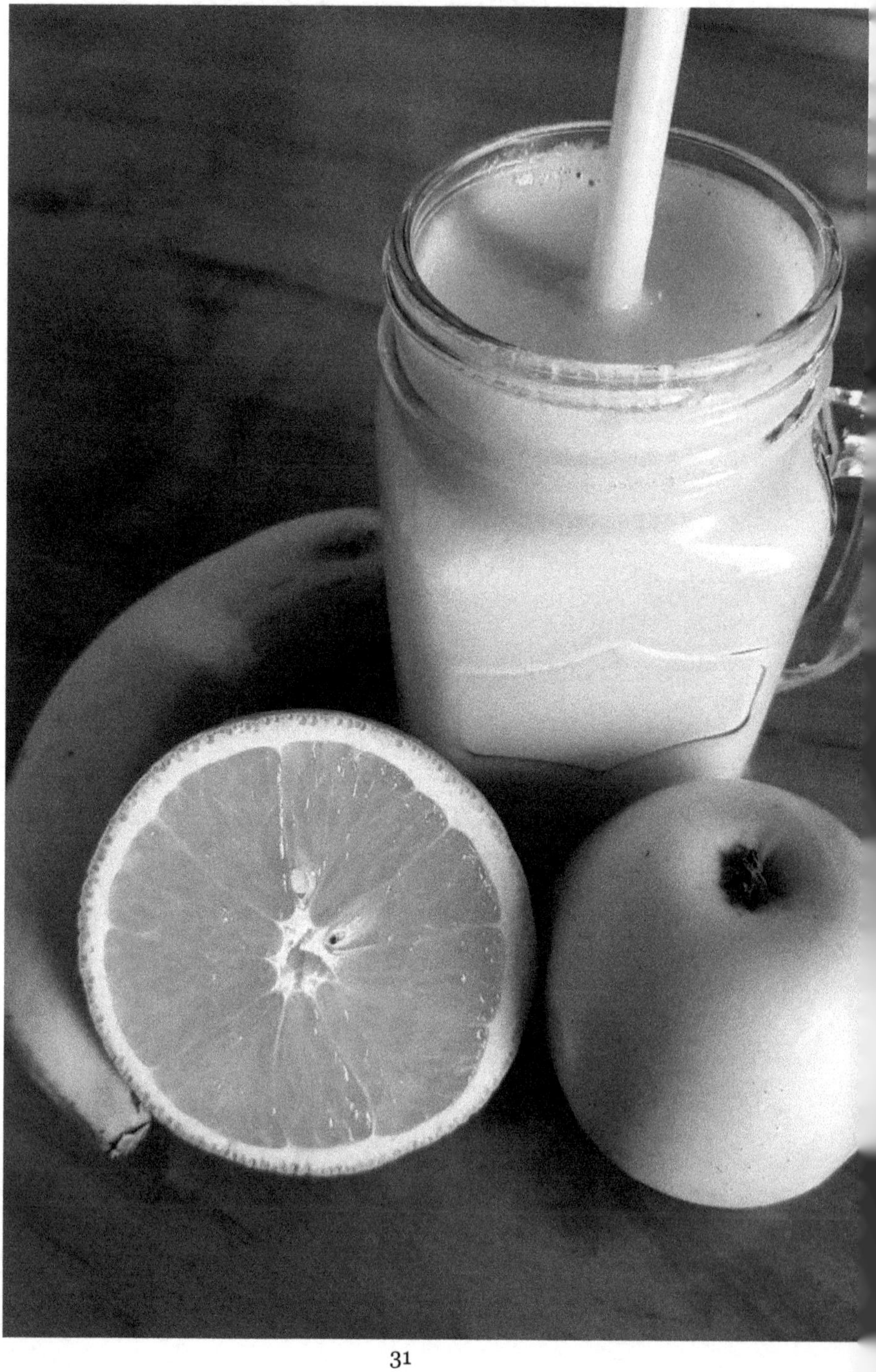

Blueberry And Spinach Shake

Time To Prepare: five minutes

Time to Cook: 0 minutes

Yield: Servings 2

Ingredients:

- 1 cup of low-fat Greek yogurt (not necessary)
- 1 cup of organic blueberries (or washed if non-organic)
- 1/2 cup of spinach
- ice cubes to the desired concentration

Directions:

1. Put in ingredients together in a blender until the desired smoothness is achieved and then serve in a tall glass.
2. Drizzle a few fresh berries on top if you prefer!

Nutritional Info: Calories: 233 kcal ‖ Protein: 10.68 g ‖ Fat: 5.38 g ‖ Carbohydrates: 37.13 g

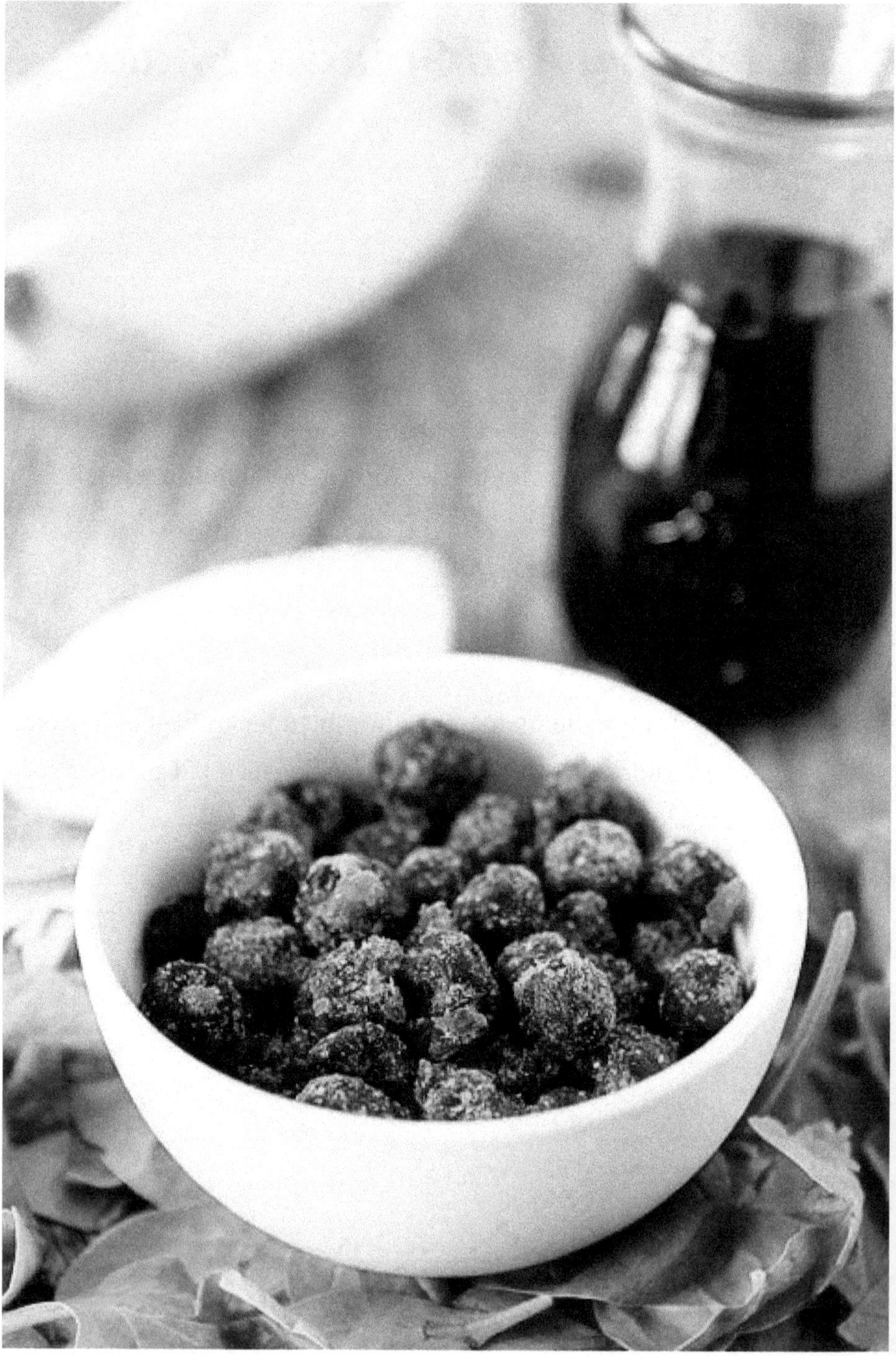

Blueberry Lime Juice

Time To Prepare: five minutes
Time to Cook: five minutes
Yield: Servings 4

Ingredients:

- 1 cup fresh blueberries
- Water to cover contents
- Zest and juice of 1 lime

Directions:

1. Put ingredients in a mesh steamer basket for instant pot. Put in pot.
2. Pour in water to immerse contents.
3. Secure the lid. Cook on HIGH pressure five minutes.
4. When done, depressurize swiftly.
5. Remove steamer basket. Discard cooked produce.
6. Let flavored water cool. Chill completely before you serve.

Nutritional Info: Calories: 86 ‖ Fat: 0g ‖ Carbohydrates: 22g ‖ Protein: 0g

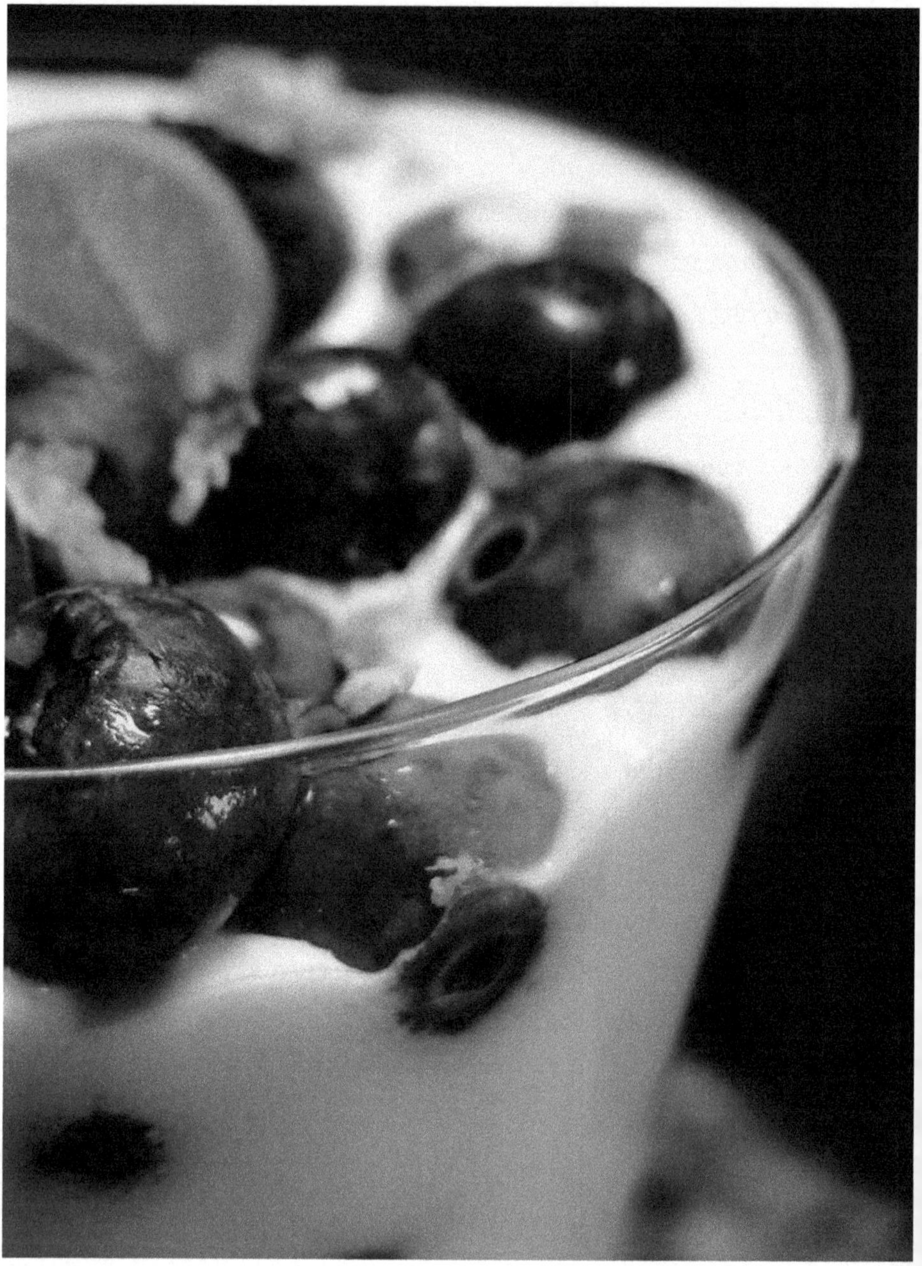

Blueberry Matcha Smoothie

Time To Prepare: five minutes
Time to Cook: 0 minutes
Yield: Servings 2

Ingredients:

- ¼ Teaspoon Ground Cinnamon
- ¼ Teaspoon Ground Ginger
- 1 Banana
- 1 Tablespoon Chia Seeds
- 1 Tablespoon Matcha Powder
- 2 Cups Almond Milk
- 2 Cups Blueberries, Frozen
- 2 Tablespoons Protein Powder, Optional
- A Pinch Sea Salt

Directions:

Blend all ingredients until the desired smoothness is achieved.

Nutritional Info: Calories: 208 ‖ Protein: 8.7 Grams ‖ Fat: 5.7 Grams ‖ Carbohydrates: 31 Grams

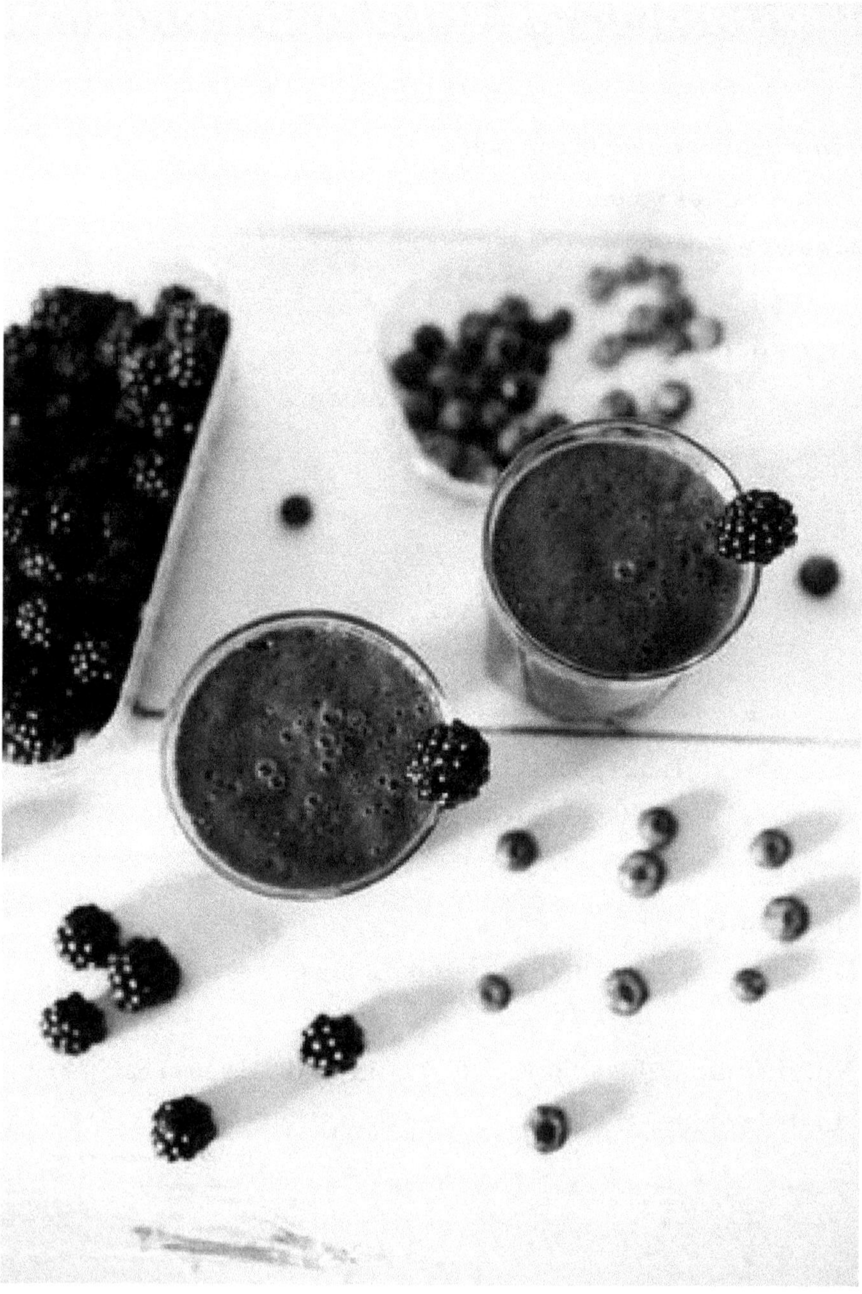

Blueberry Pomegranate Smoothie

Time To Prepare: five minutes
Time to Cook: 0 minutes
Yield: Servings 2

Ingredients:

- ¼ cup of canned coconut milk
- 1 cup of pomegranate juice, unsweetened
- 1 tbsp. of hemp seeds
- 2 cup of frozen blueberries
- 6 to 8 ice cubes

Directions:

1. Mix the smoothie ingredients in your high-speed blender.
2. Pulse the ingredients a few times to cut them up.
3. Combine the mixture on the highest speed setting for thirty to 60 seconds.
4. Pour into glasses and serve.

Nutritional Info: Calories: 282 kcal ‖ Protein: 5.64 g ‖ Fat: 13.8 g ‖ Carbohydrates: 37.75 g

Blueberry Smoothie

Time To Prepare: ten minutes
Time to Cook: 0 minutes
Yield: Servings 1

Ingredients:

- 1 banana, peeled
- 1 tbsp. almond butter
- 1 tsp. maca powder
- 1/2 cup almond milk, unsweetened
- 1/2 cup blueberries
- 1/2 cup water
- 1/4 tsp. ground cinnamon
- 2 handfuls baby spinach

Directions:

1. In your blender, combine the spinach with the banana, blueberries, almond butter, cinnamon, maca powder, water, and milk.
2. Pulse thoroughly, pour into a glass, before you serve. Enjoy!

Nutritional Info: Calories: 341 ‖ Fat: 12 g ‖ Protein: 10 g ‖ Carbohydrates: 54 g ‖ Fiber: 12 g

SIDES

Citrus Couscous with Herb

Time To Prepare: five minutes

Time to Cook: fifteen minutes

Yield: Servings 2

Ingredients:

- ¼ cup of water
- ¼ orange, chopped
- ½ teaspoon butter
- 1 teaspoon Italian seasonings
- 1/3 cup couscous
- 1/3 teaspoon salt
- 4 tablespoons orange juice

Directions:

1. Pour water and orange juice in the pan.
2. Put in orange, Italian seasoning, and salt.
3. Bring the liquid to boil and take it off the heat.
4. Put in butter and couscous. Stir thoroughly and close the lid.
5. Leave the couscous rest for about ten minutes.

Nutritional Info: Calories 149 ‖ Fat: 1.9 ‖ Fiber: 2.1 ‖ Carbs: 28.5 ‖ Protein: 4.1

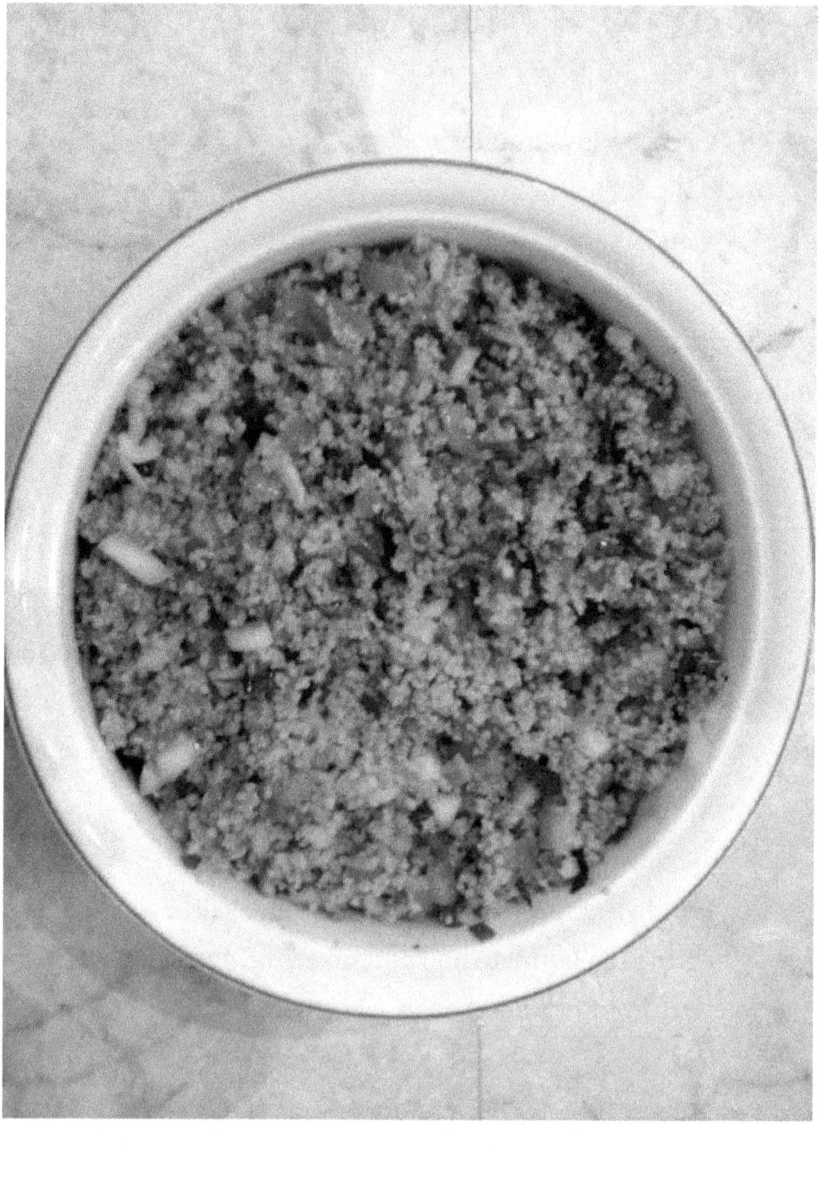

Cool Garbanzo and Spinach Beans

Time To Prepare: 5-ten minutes

Time to Cook: 0 minute

Yield: Servings 4

Ingredients:

- ½ onion, diced
- ½ teaspoon cumin
- 1 tablespoon olive oil
- 10 ounces spinach, chopped
- 12 ounces garbanzo beans

Directions:

1. Take a frying pan and put in olive oil
2. Put it on moderate to low heat
3. Put in onions, garbanzo and cook for five minutes
4. Mix in cumin, garbanzo beans, spinach and flavor with sunflower seeds
5. Use a spoon to smash gently
6. Cook meticulously
7. Serve and enjoy!

Nutritional Info: ‖ Calories: 90 ‖ Fat: 4g ‖ Carbohydrates:11g ‖ Protein:4g

Couscous Salad

Time To Prepare: ten minutes
Time to Cook: six minutes
Yield: Servings 4

Ingredients:

- ¼ teaspoon ground black pepper
- ¾ teaspoon ground coriander
- ½ teaspoon salt
- ¼ teaspoon paprika
- ¼ teaspoon turmeric
- 1 tablespoon butter
- 2 oz. chickpeas, canned, drained
- 1 cup fresh arugula, chopped
- 2 oz. sun-dried tomatoes, chopped
- 1 oz. Feta cheese, crumbled
- 1 tablespoon canola oil
- 1/3 cup couscous
- 1/3 cup chicken stock

Directions:

1. Bring the chicken stock to boil.
2. Put in couscous, ground black pepper, ground coriander, salt, paprika, and turmeric. Put in chickpeas and butter. Mix the mixture well and close the lid.

3. Allow the couscous soak the hot chicken stock for about six minutes.

4. In the meantime, in the mixing container mix together arugula, sun-dried tomatoes, and Feta cheese.

5. Put in cooked couscous mixture and canola oil.

6. Mix up the salad well.

Nutritional Info: Calories 18 ‖ Fat: 9 ‖ Fiber: 3.6 ‖ Carbs: 21.1 ‖ Protein: 6

Creamy Polenta

Time To Prepare: 8 minutes

Time to Cook: forty-five minutes

Yield: Servings 4

Ingredients:

- ½ cup cream
- 1 ½ cup water
- 1 cup polenta
- 1/3 cup Parmesan, grated
- 2 cups chicken stock

Directions:

1. Put polenta in the pot.
2. Put in water, chicken stock, cream, and Parmesan. Mix up polenta well.
3. Then preheat oven to 355F.
4. Cook polenta in your oven for about forty-five minutes.
5. Mix up the cooked meal with the help of the spoon cautiously before you serve.

Nutritional Info: Calories 208 ‖ Fat: 5.3 ‖ Fiber: 1 ‖ Carbs: 32.2 ‖ Protein: 8

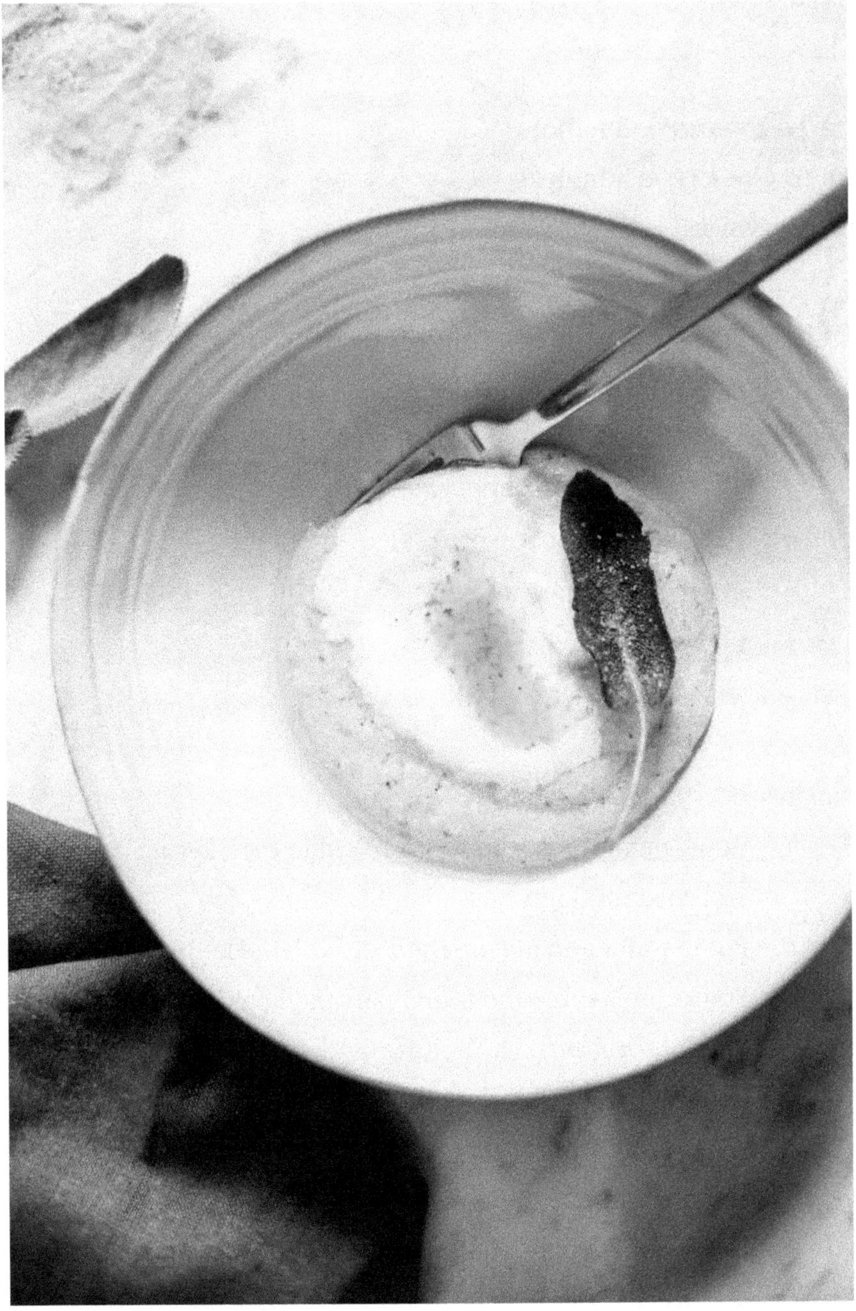

Crispy Corn

Time To Prepare: 8 minutes
Time to Cook: five minutes
Yield: Servings 3

Ingredients:

- ½ teaspoon ground paprika
- ½ teaspoon salt
- ¾ teaspoon chili pepper
- 1 cup corn kernels
- 1 tablespoon coconut flour
- 1 tablespoon water
- 3 tablespoons canola oil

Directions:

1. In the mixing container, mix together corn kernels with salt and coconut flour.
2. Put in water and mix up the corn with the help of the spoon.
3. Pour canola oil in the frying pan and heat it.
4. Put in corn kernels mixture and roast it for about four minutes. Stir it occasionally.
5. When the corn kernels are crispy, move them in the plate and dry with the paper towel's help.
6. Put in chili pepper and ground paprika. Mix up well.

Nutritional Info: Calories 179 ‖ Fat: fifteen ‖ Fiber: 2.4 ‖ Carbs: 11.3 ‖ Protein: 2.1

SAUCES AND DRESSINGS

Bean Potato Spread

Time To Prepare: twenty-five minutes

Time to Cook: 0 minutes

Yield: Servings 7-8

Ingredients:

- ¼ cup sesame paste
- ½ teaspoon cumin, ground
- 1 cup garbanzo beans, drained and washed
- 1 tablespoon olive oil
- 2 tablespoons lime juice
- 2 tablespoons water
- 4 cups cooked sweet potatoes, peeled and chopped
- 5 garlic cloves, minced
- A pinch of salt

Directions:

1. Throw all the ingredients into a blender and blend to make a smooth mix.
2. Move to a container.
3. Serve with carrot, celery, or veggie sticks.

Nutritional Info: Calories 156 ‖ Fat: 3g ‖ Carbohydrates: 10g ‖ Fiber: 6g ‖ Protein: 8g

Cashew Ginger Dip

Time To Prepare: five minutes

Time to Cook: 0 minutes

Yield: Servings 1

Ingredients:

- ¼ cup filtered water
- ¼ teaspoon salt
- ½ teaspoon ground ginger
- 1 cup cashews, soaked in water for about twenty minutes and drained
- 1 tablespoon extra-virgin olive oil
- 1 teaspoon lemon juice
- 2 garlic cloves
- 2 teaspoons coconut aminos
- Pinch cayenne pepper

Directions:

1. In a blender or food processor, put together the cashews, garlic, water, olive oil, aminos, lemon juice, ginger, salt, and cayenne pepper.
2. Put in the mix in a container.
3. Cover and place in your fridge until chilled. You can use store it for 4-5 days in your fridge.

Nutritional Info: Calories 124 ‖ Fat: 9g ‖ Carbohydrates: 5g ‖ Fiber: 1g ‖ Protein: 3g

SNACKS

Avocado Hummus

Time To Prepare: fifteen minutes

Time to Cook: 0 minutes

Yield: Servings 4

Ingredients:

- .25 cup Sunflower seeds
- .25 cup Tahini
- .25 tsp. Pepper
- .5 cup Cilantro
- .5 cup Coconut oil
- .5 Lemon juice
- .5 tsp. Salt
- 1 clove pressed garlic
- 3 Avocados
- 5 tsp. Cumin

Directions:

1. Halve the avocados, take off the pits, then spoon out the flesh.
2. Put all together ingredients in a blender and stir until super smooth.

3. Put in water, lemon juice, or oil if you need to loosen the mixture bit.

Nutritional Info: ǁ Calories: 651 kcal ǁ Protein: 9.62 g ǁ Fat: 64.05 g ǁ Carbohydrates: 19.95 g

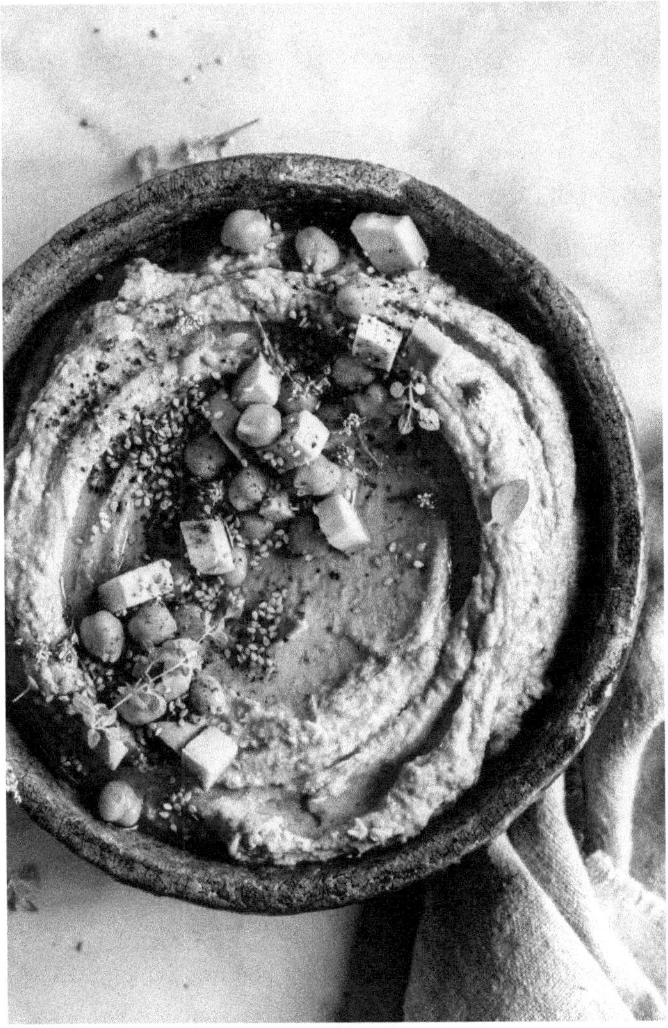

Avocado with Tomatoes and Cucumber

Time To Prepare: ten minutes

Time to Cook: 0 minutes

Yield: Servings 2

Ingredients:

- ¼ cup cilantro
- ¼ cup olives – to your choice
- ½ red onion
- 1 cucumber
- 1 lemon
- 1 Tbsp. turmeric
- 1/8 cup parsley
- 2 avocados
- 4 Roma tomatoes
- Salt and pepper – to your taste

Directions:

1. Dice the tomatoes, cucumber, avocado, and olives.
2. Cut the cilantro, parsley, and onion.
3. Put in the above ingredients into a container.
4. Squeeze the lemon juice then put in to the vegetables.
5. Put in olive oil, turmeric, salt, and pepper.
6. Toss thoroughly.

7. Consume instantly after putting in lemon juice and olive oil.

8. If you prefer to consume the salad later, put in the dressing instantly before consuming it.

Nutritional Info: ‖ Calories: 480 kcal ‖ Protein: 11.57 g ‖ Fat: 35.27 g ‖ Carbohydrates: 39.77 g

Baked Veggie Turmeric Nuggets

Time To Prepare: ten minutes
Time to Cook: twenty-five minutes
Yield: Servings 24

Ingredients:

- ¼ tsp. Black pepper powder
- ¼ tsp. Sea salt
- ½ cup Almond meal
- ½ tsp. Turmeric powder
- 1 big Whole egg
- 1 cup Chopped carrots
- 1 tsp. Minced garlic
- 2 cups Broccoli florets
- 2 cups Cauliflower florets

Directions:

1. Preheat your oven to 400°F.
2. Get a parchment-lined baking sheet ready.
3. Pour cauliflower, turmeric, broccoli, carrots, black pepper, garlic, and sea salt in the blender and blitz until it's smooth.
4. Pour in the egg and almond meal and stir until it's blended.
5. Pour the paste into a mixing container. Scoop out a small amount onto your hand and make a circular disc. Put this disc on the baking sheet and repeat the pulse until the mixing container is empty.

6. Slide into the oven then bake for minimum fifteen minutes on one before flipping and baking for about ten minutes on the other side.

7. Serve with a side of Paleo ranch sauce.

Nutritional Info: ‖ Calories: 12 kcal ‖ Protein: 0.88 g ‖ Fat: 0.52 g ‖ Carbohydrates: 1.12 g

Berry Delight

Time To Prepare: fifteen minutes

Time to Cook: 0 minutes

Yield: Servings 6

Ingredients:

- ¼ cup of raw honey
- 1 cup of fresh organic blackberries
- 1 cup of fresh organic blueberries
- 1 cup of fresh organic raspberries
- 1 tablespoon of cinnamon

Directions:

1. Mix all the berries together in a big container, put in in the honey, and slowly stir.
2. Drizzle with the cinnamon.

Nutritional Info: ‖ Total Carbohydrates: 20g ‖ Fiber: 3g ‖ Net Carbohydrates: ‖ Protein: 1g ‖ Total Fat: 0g ‖ Calories: 78

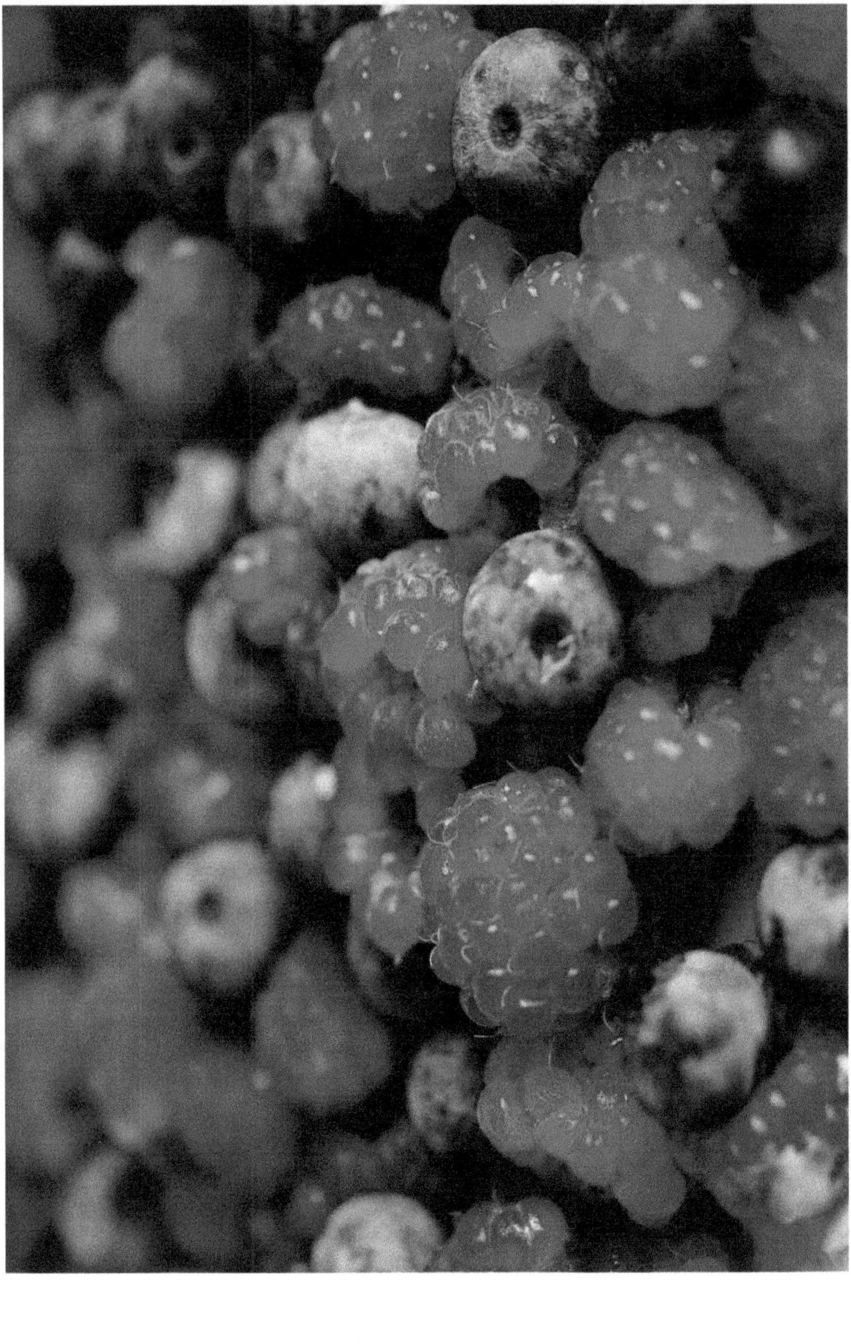

Berry Energy bites

Time To Prepare: ten minutes
Time to Cook: 0 minutes
Yield: Servings 6

Ingredients:

- ¼ cup of dried blueberries
- ½ - 1 cup of almond milk
- ½ cup of coconut flour
- 1 tablespoon of coconut sugar
- 1 teaspoon of cinnamon

Directions:

1. In a huge mixing container, put together the coconut flour, cinnamon, coconut sugar, and blueberries, and mix thoroughly.
2. Put in the almond milk slowly until a firm dough is formed.
3. Form into bite-sized balls and place in your fridge for thirty minutes so they can harden up.
4. Store leftovers in your fridge.

Nutritional Info: ‖ Total Carbohydrates: 18g ‖ Fiber: 1g ‖ Net Carbohydrates: ‖ Protein: 1g ‖ Total Fat: 1g ‖ Calories: 80

Blueberry & Chia Flax Seed Pudding

Time To Prepare: ten minutes

Time to Cook: fifteen minutes

Yield: Servings 4

Ingredients:

- ¼ cup of blueberries
- 2 cups of almond milk
- 3 tablespoons of chia seeds
- 3 tablespoons of ground flaxseed

Directions:

1. Warm a pan on moderate heat then put all together of the ingredients apart from the blueberries.
2. Stir all the ingredients until the pudding is thick, this will take around three minutes.
3. Place the pudding into a container then top with blueberries.

Nutritional Info: ‖ Total Carbohydrates: 23g ‖ Fiber: 12g ‖ Net Carbohydrates: ‖ Protein: 7g ‖ Total Fat: 15g ‖ Calories: 243

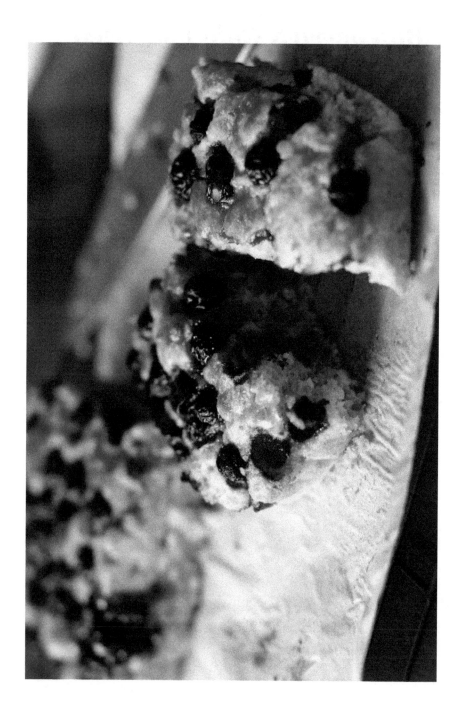

Boiled Okra and Squash

Time To Prepare: five minutes

Time to Cook: five minutes

Yield: Servings 1

Ingredients:

- ½ cup of okra, cut in 1" cubes
- ½ cup of squash, cut in 1" cubes
- 1 clove garlic, minced
- 2/3 cup Vegetable stock or fish stock, plain water may be used as well
- Salt to taste

Directions:

1. Boil the liquid in high heat.
2. Put in the okra and squash. Bring to its boiling point. Put in the garlic. Reduced the heat and simmer for minimum five minutes or until the squash is soft.
3. Put in salt to taste and serve hot.

Nutritional Info: ‖ Calories: 117 kcal ‖ Protein: 8.2 g ‖ Fat: 6.25 g ‖ Carbohydrates: 7.82 g

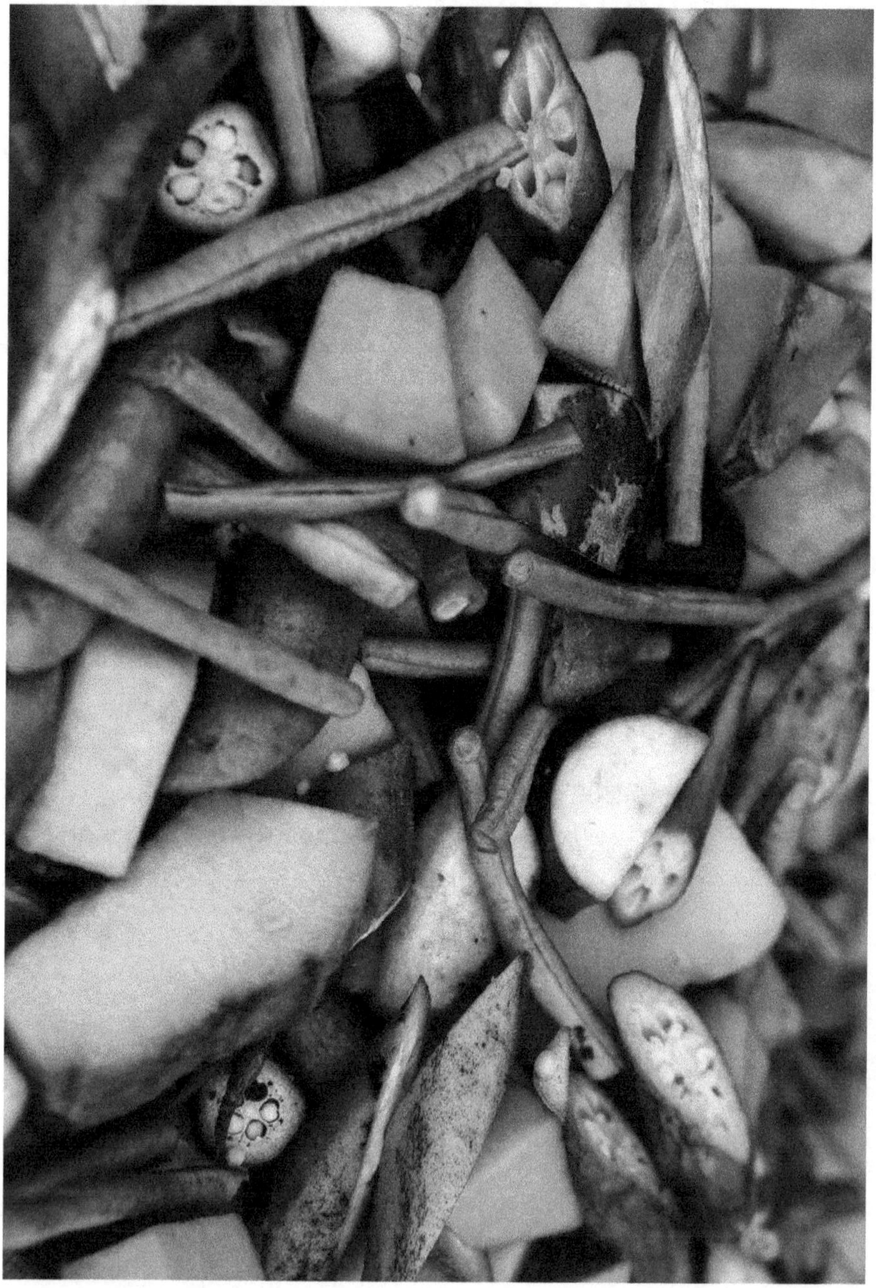

SOUPS AND STEWS

Carrot Broccoli Stew

Time To Prepare: ten minutes

Time to Cook: forty-five minutes

Yield: Servings 3

Ingredients:

- 1 cup Broccoli, florets
- 1 cup Carrots, cut
- 1 cup Heavy Cream
- 3 cups Chicken broth
- Salt and black pepper to taste

Directions:

1. Put in florets, cream, carrots, salt, and chicken broth; toss thoroughly. Secure the lid and cook on Meat/Stew mode for forty minutes on High. When ready, do a quick pressure release.
2. Move into serving bowls and drizzle black pepper on top.

Nutritional Info: Calories 145 ‖ Protein: 1.5g ‖ Carbs: 1.2g

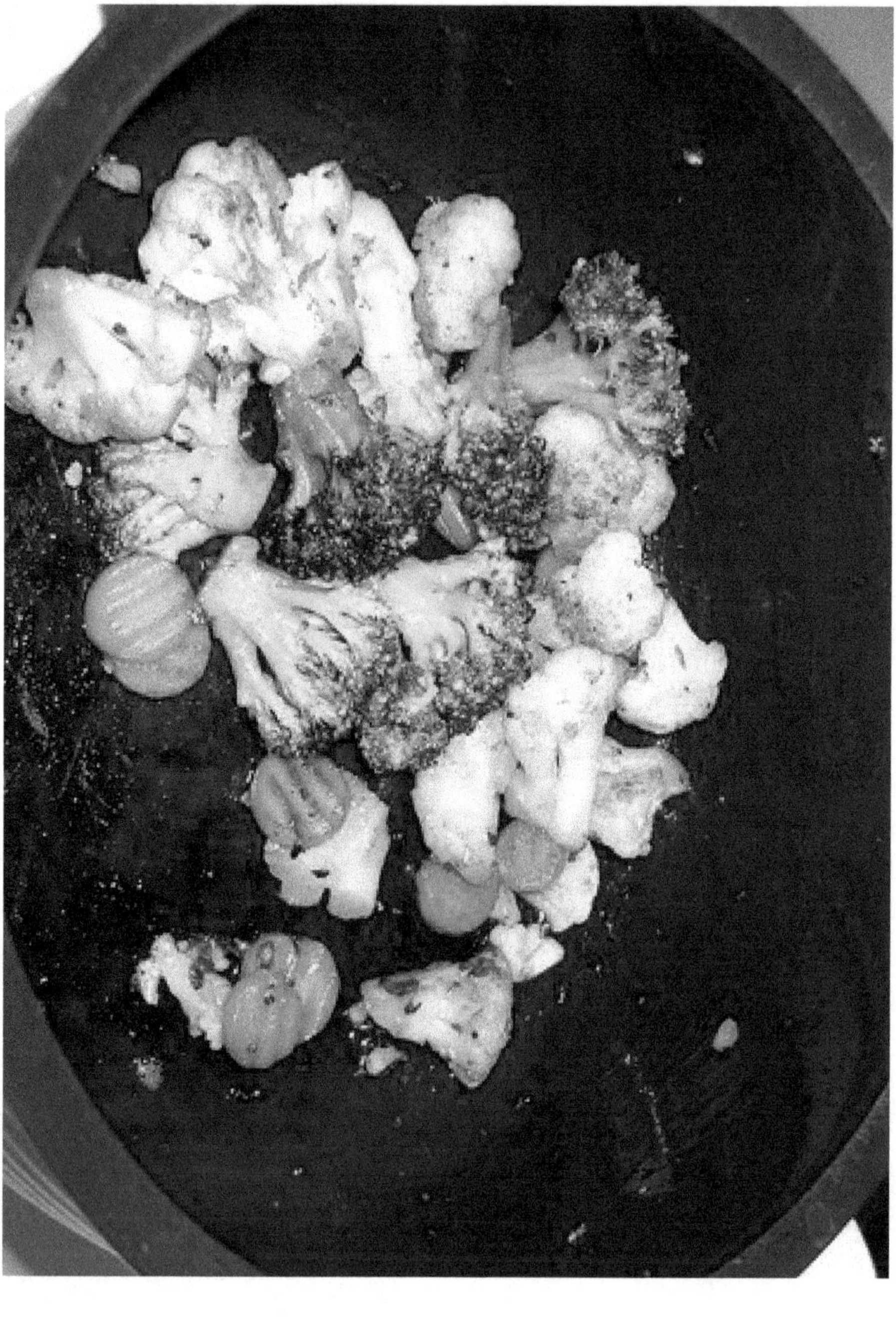

Carrot, Ginger & Turmeric Soup

Time To Prepare: fifteen minutes
Time to Cook: forty minutes
Yield: Servings 8

Ingredients:

- ¼ cup full-fat unsweetened coconut milk
- ¾ pound carrots, peeled and chopped
- 1 sweet yellow onion, chopped
- 1 teaspoon ground turmeric
- 2 cloves garlic, chopped
- 2 teaspoons grated ginger
- 6 cups vegetable broth
- Pinch of sea salt & pepper, to taste

Directions:

1. Put in all the ingredients minus the coconut milk to a stockpot on moderate heat and bring to its boiling point. Reduce to a simmer and cook for forty minutes or until the carrots are soft.
2. Use an immersion blender and blend the soup until the desired smoothness is achieved. Mix in the coconut milk.
3. Enjoy immediately and freeze any remainings.

Nutritional Info: Calories: 73 ǁ Carbohydrates: 7g ǁ Fiber: 2g Net ǁ Carbohydrates: 5g ǁ Fat: 3g ǁ Protein: 4g

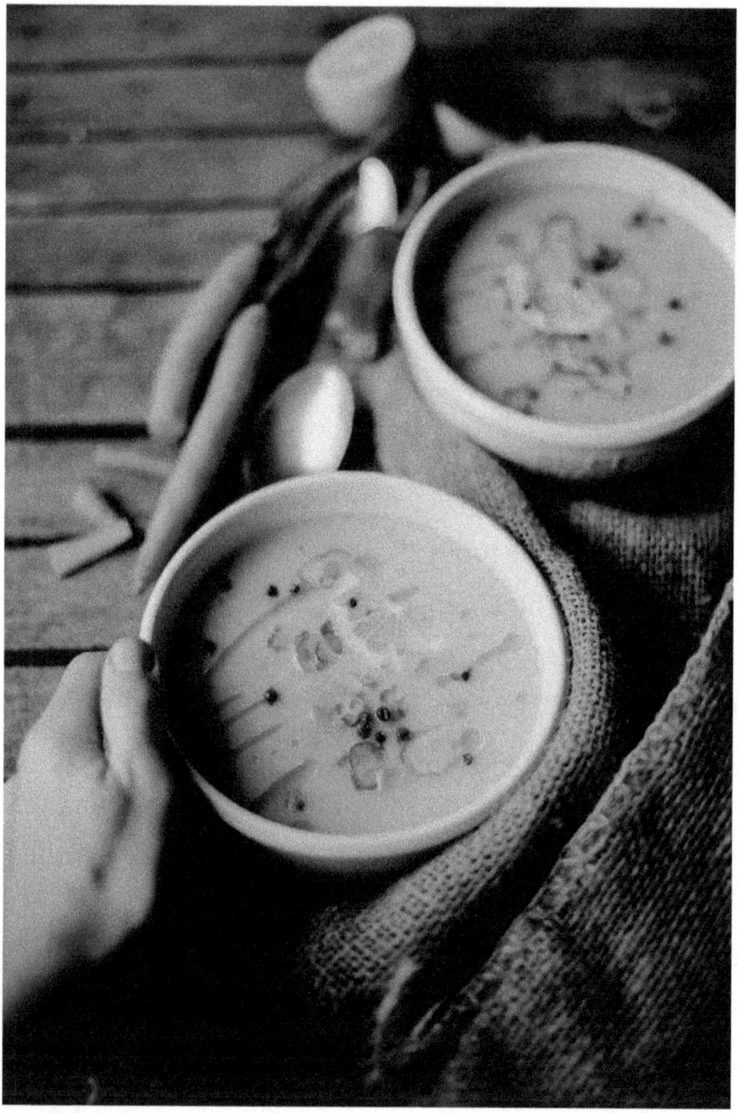

Cauliflower And Clam Chowder

Time To Prepare: ten minutes
Time to Cook: ten minutes
Yield: Servings 6

Ingredients:

- ½ teaspoon dried thyme
- 1 small yellow onion
- 1½ cups heavy whipping cream
- 3 (6.5-ounce / 184-g) cans chopped clams
- 3 tablespoons butter
- 4 cups chopped cauliflower
- From the cupboard:
- Salt and freshly ground black pepper, to taste

Directions:

1. Split the clams and clam juice into two bowls. Thin the clam juice with water to make 2 cups of juice.
2. Place the onion and butter in an instant pot and press the Sauté bottom, then sauté for a couple of minutes or until the onion is translucent.
3. Put in the clam juice and cauliflower into the instant pot. Place the lid on and press the Manual button, and set the temperature to 375°F (190°C), then cook for five minutes.
4. Quick Release the pressure, then open the lid and mix in the heavy cream and clams.

5. Push the Sauté bottom and cook for about three minutes or until the clams are opaque and firm, then drizzle with thyme, salt, and black pepper. Stir to mix thoroughly.
6. Ladle the chowder in a big container and serve warm.

Nutritional Info: calories: 252 ‖ total fat: 17.3g ‖ total carbs: 8.9g ‖ fiber: 2.1g ‖ net carbs: 6.8g ‖ protein: 17.1g

Cauliflower, Coconut Milk, And Shrimp Soup

Time To Prepare: five minutes

Time to Cook: 2 hours and fifteen minutes

Yield: Servings 4

Ingredients:

- 1 (13.5-ounce / 383-g) can unsweetened full-fat coconut milk
- 1 cup shrimp, peeled, deveined, tail off, and cooked
- 1 cup water
- 2 cups riced cauliflower
- 2 tablespoons chopped fresh cilantro leaves, divided
- 2 tablespoons red curry paste
- From the cupboard:
- Salt and freshly ground black pepper, to taste

Directions:

1. Put in the riced cauliflower, red curry paste, coconut milk, 1 tablespoon cilantro, water, then drizzle with salt and black pepper. Combine the mixture to blend well.
2. Place the slow cooker lid on and cook on HIGH for about two hours.
3. Place the shrimp on a clean working surface, then drizzle salt and black pepper to season.

4. Place the shrimp in the slow cooker and cook for fifteen minutes more.

5. Move the soup into a big container and top with the rest of the cilantro leaves before you serve.

Nutritional Info: calories: 268 ‖ total fat: 21.3g ‖ total carbs: 7.8g ‖ fiber: 3.2g ‖ net carbs: 4.6g ‖ protein: 16.1g

Celery Soup

Time To Prepare: ten minutes
Time to Cook: twenty minutes
Yield: Servings 4

Ingredients:

- ½ cup brown onion, chopped
- ½ cup full-fat milk
- ½ pound with Salsiccia links, casing removed and cut
- ½ teaspoon dried chili flakes
- ½ teaspoon ground black pepper
- 1 carrot, chopped
- 1 garlic clove, pressed
- 2 teaspoon coconut oil
- 3 cups celery, chopped
- 3 cups roasted vegetable broth
- Kosher salt, to taste

Directions:

1. Simply throw all of the above ingredients into your Instant Pot; gently stir until blended.
2. Secure the lid. Choose "Soup/Broth" mode and High pressure; cook for about twenty-five minutes. Once cooking is complete, use a quick pressure release; cautiously remove the lid.
3. Ladle into four soup bowls and serve hot. Enjoy!

Nutritional Info: 150 Calories ‖ 5.9g Fat ‖ 5.9g Total Carbs ‖ 16.4g Protein ‖ 4.1g Sugars

Cheesy Broccoli Soup

Time To Prepare: five minutes
Time to Cook: twenty minutes
Yield: Servings 4

Ingredients:

- 1 cup broccoli, cut into florets
- 1 cup chicken broth
- 1 cup heavy whipping cream
- 1 cup shredded Cheddar cheese, plus more for topping
- 2 tablespoons butter
- From the cupboard:
- Salt and freshly ground black pepper, to taste

Directions:

1. Place the butter in a deep cooking pan, and melt on moderate heat.
2. Put in and sauté the broccoli for four to five minutes or until tender.
3. Stir in the chicken broth and heavy whipping cream over the broccoli, and drizzle with salt and black pepper. Cook for approximately fifteen minutes or until the soup is smooth and thickened. Keep stirring during the cooking.
4. Lower the heat to low and gently fold in the Cheddar cheese. Keep stirring until well blended.

5. Ladle the soup into a big container. Spread more cheese over the soup before you serve.

Nutritional Info: calories: 386 ‖ total fat: 37.3g ‖ total carbs: 3.8g ‖ fiber: 1.1g ‖ net carbs: 2.7g ‖ protein: 9.8g

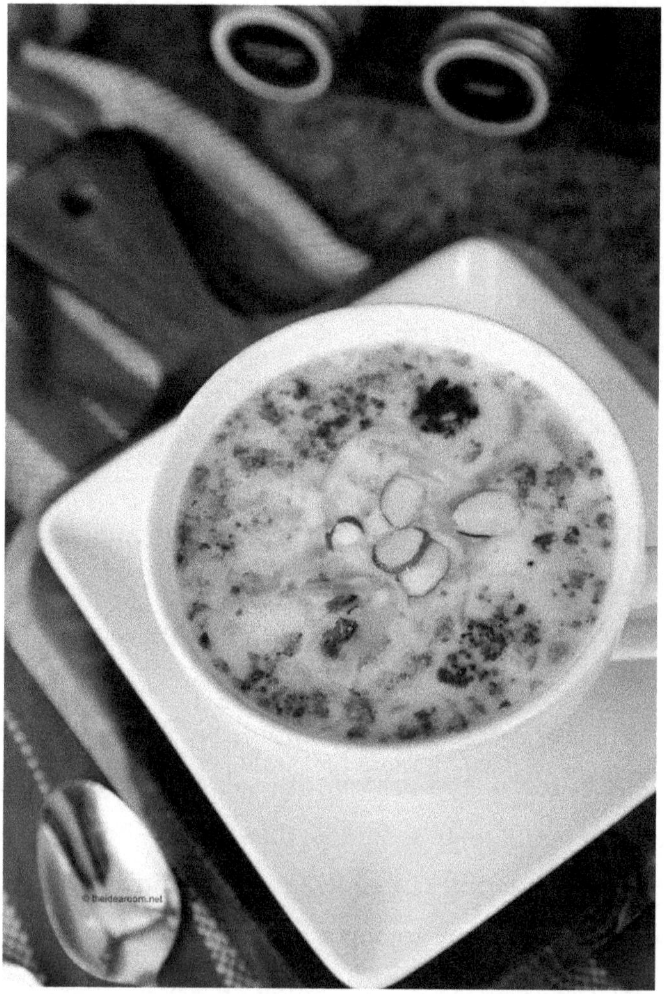
© theidearoom.net

Cheesy Chicken Soup

Time To Prepare: twenty minutes

Time to Cook: 33-40 minutes

Yield: Servings 6

Ingredients:

- ¼ teaspoon black pepper
- ½ cup shredded cheddar cheese
- ½ teaspoon cumin
- ½ teaspoon salt
- 1 cup whipped cream cheese
- 1 tablespoon coconut oil, for cooking
- 1 teaspoon chili powder
- 1 yellow onion, chopped
- 2 boneless, skinless chicken breasts
- 2 cloves garlic, chopped
- 2 cups chicken broth
- 2 cups water

Directions:

1. Heat a big frying pan on moderate heat with a ½ tablespoon of the coconut oil.
2. Brown the chicken breasts until thoroughly cooked. Set aside.

3. Put in the garlic and onion to a big stockpot with the rest of the 1 tablespoon of the coconut oil and sauté until translucent over low to moderate heat. This should take about three to five minutes.
4. Put in this chicken broth and water.
5. Whisk in the cream cheese and keep whisking over low to moderate heat until blended.
6. Put in in the spices and bring to its boiling point.
7. While the water is boiling, chop the chicken into bite-sized pieces and put in to the stockpot.
8. Reduce to a simmer and cook for half an hour.
9. Mix in the cheddar cheese before you serve.

Nutritional Info: Calories: 157 ‖ Carbohydrates: 5g ‖ Fiber: 1g Net ‖ Carbohydrates: 4g ‖ Fat: 7g ‖ Protein: 17g

Cheesy Tomato And Basil Soup

Time To Prepare: five minutes
Time to Cook: fifteen minutes
Yield: Servings 12

Ingredients:

- ¼ teaspoon ground black pepper
- 1 tablespoon dried basil
- 1 teaspoon dried oregano
- 1 teaspoon salt
- 2 (14 ounces / 397 g) canned whole tomatoes, diced
- 2 garlic cloves, minced
- 2 tablespoons coconut oil
- 4 cups chicken broth
- 4 ounces (113 g) red onions, finely diced
- 5 ounces (142 g) grated Parmesan cheese, plus more for decoration
- 8 ounces (227 g) cream cheese, softened
- Fresh basil, chopped, for decoration

Directions:

1. Grease a nonstick frying pan with coconut oil, and sauté the onions, basil, oregano, and garlic in the frying pan for about four minutes or until aromatic.

2. Put in the cream cheese and fully whisk until no clump, then fold in the chicken broth, and put in the cheese, tomatoes, salt, and pepper. Stir to blend well.

3. Cover the lid and bring them to a simmer on moderate heat for eight minutes. Move the soup into a blender, then blitz until it becomes thick.

4. Lightly pour the soup into a big serving container and sprinkle with Parmesan cheese and basil as decorate.

Nutritional Info: calories: 146 ‖ total fat: 12g ‖ net carbs: 3g ‖ fiber: 1g ‖ protein: 6g

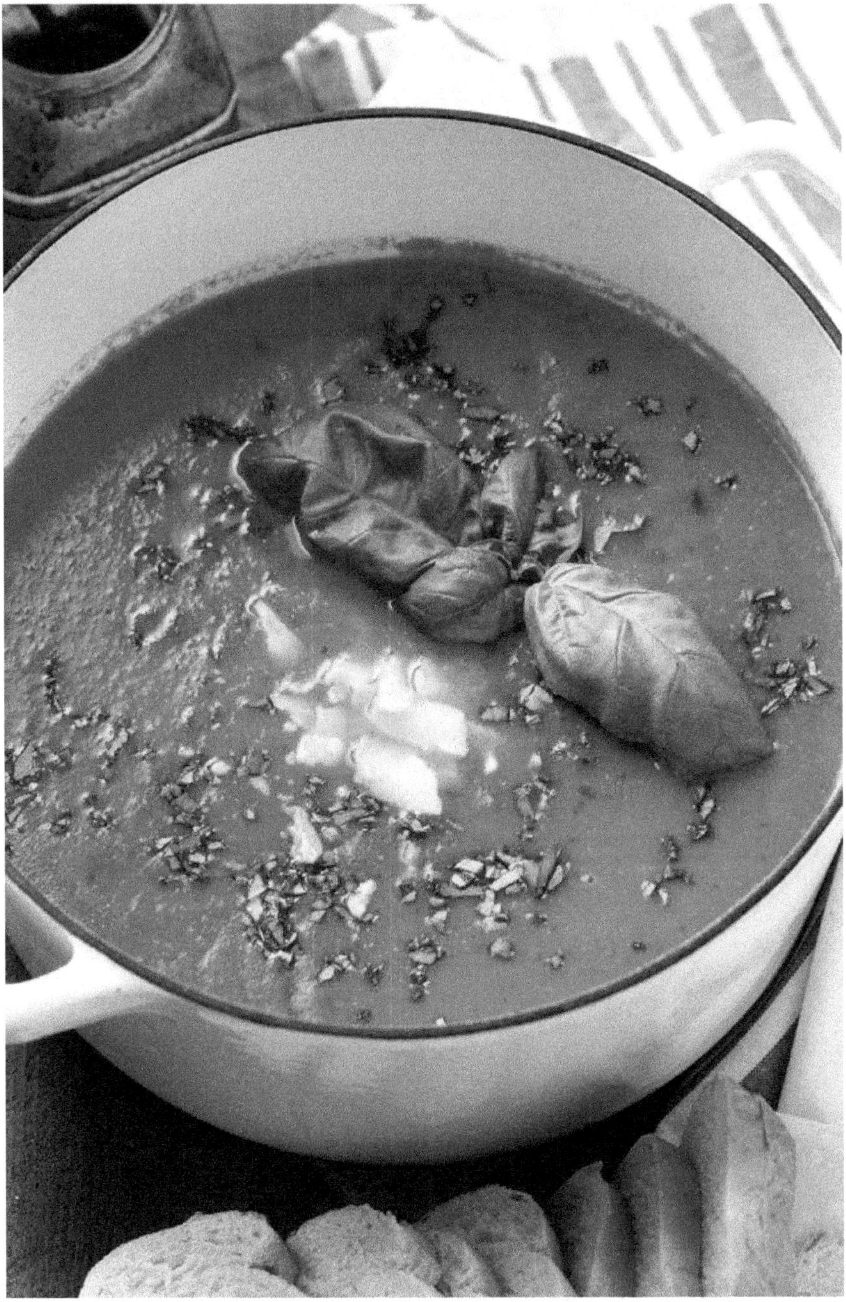

Chicken And Cauliflower Curry Stew

Time To Prepare: fifteen minutes
Time to Cook: 4 hours
Yield: Servings 7

Ingredients:

- ¼ cup fresh cilantro, chopped
- ⅓ cup coconut oil
- 1 green bell pepper, chopped
- 1 pound (454 g) cauliflower, chopped into little pieces
- 1.5pounds (680 g) skinless, boneless chicken thighs, cut into bite-sized pieces
- 14 ounces (397 g) unsweetened coconut milk
- 2 tablespoons curry powder
- 2 tablespoons ginger garlic paste
- Salt and ground black pepper, to taste

Directions:

1. Warm half of the coconut oil in a nonstick frying pan on moderate heat, then sauté the garlic ginger paste and curry powder for a minutes or until aromatic.
2. Put in the chicken pieces, and drizzle with salt and pepper. sauté for another ten minutes or until the chicken is mildly

browned. Remove from the frying pan and set aside in warm.

3. Warm another half of coconut oil in the frying pan, then sauté the cauliflower and bell pepper on moderate to high heat for one to two minutes.

4. Then fold in the coconut milk and reduce the heat to low. Cover with lid and stew for about forty-five minutes.

5. Drizzle with salt and pepper, then put in the sautéed chicken. Move the stew to a big platter and serve with cilantro on top as decorate.

Nutritional Info: calories: 782 ‖ total fat: 68g ‖ net carbs: 9g ‖ fiber: 5g ‖ protein: 33g

Chicken And Kale Soup

Time To Prepare: five minutes

Time to Cook: 4 hours

Yield: Servings 4

Ingredients:

- 1 (7-ounce / 198-g) bunch kale, trimmed and chopped
- 1 big chicken breast, cut into little strips
- 2 tablespoons olive oil
- 3 tablespoons fresh ginger, grated
- 6 cups chicken stock
- 6 garlic cloves, finely chopped
- From the cupboard:
- Salt and freshly ground black pepper, to taste

Directions:

1. Grease the insert of the slow cooker with olive oil.
2. Combine the chicken breast, stock, kale, ginger, garlic, ginger, salt, and black pepper in the slow cooker.
3. Place the slow cooker lid on and cook on HIGH for 4 hours.
4. Ladle the stew in a big container and serve warm.

Nutritional Info: calories: 168 ‖ total fat: 7.6g ‖ total carbs: 8.3g ‖ fiber: 2.1g ‖ net carbs: 6.2g ‖ protein: 18.7g

DESSERTS

Banana Cinnamon

Time To Prepare: two minutes
Time to Cook: 8 minutes
Yield: Servings 2-4

Ingredients:

- 1 big banana, chopped into ½ inch
- 1 tsp. cinnamon
- 2 tsp. honey

Directions:

1. In a small container, put the honey and cinnamon and mix well.
2. Heat the olive oil in a pan. Cook banana slices for a couple of minutes or until browned all over.
3. Pour honey and cinnamon mixture over the bananas and serve.

Nutritional Info: ‖ Calories: 33 kcal ‖ Protein: 1.64 g ‖ Fat: 1.52 g ‖ Carbohydrates: 3.43 g

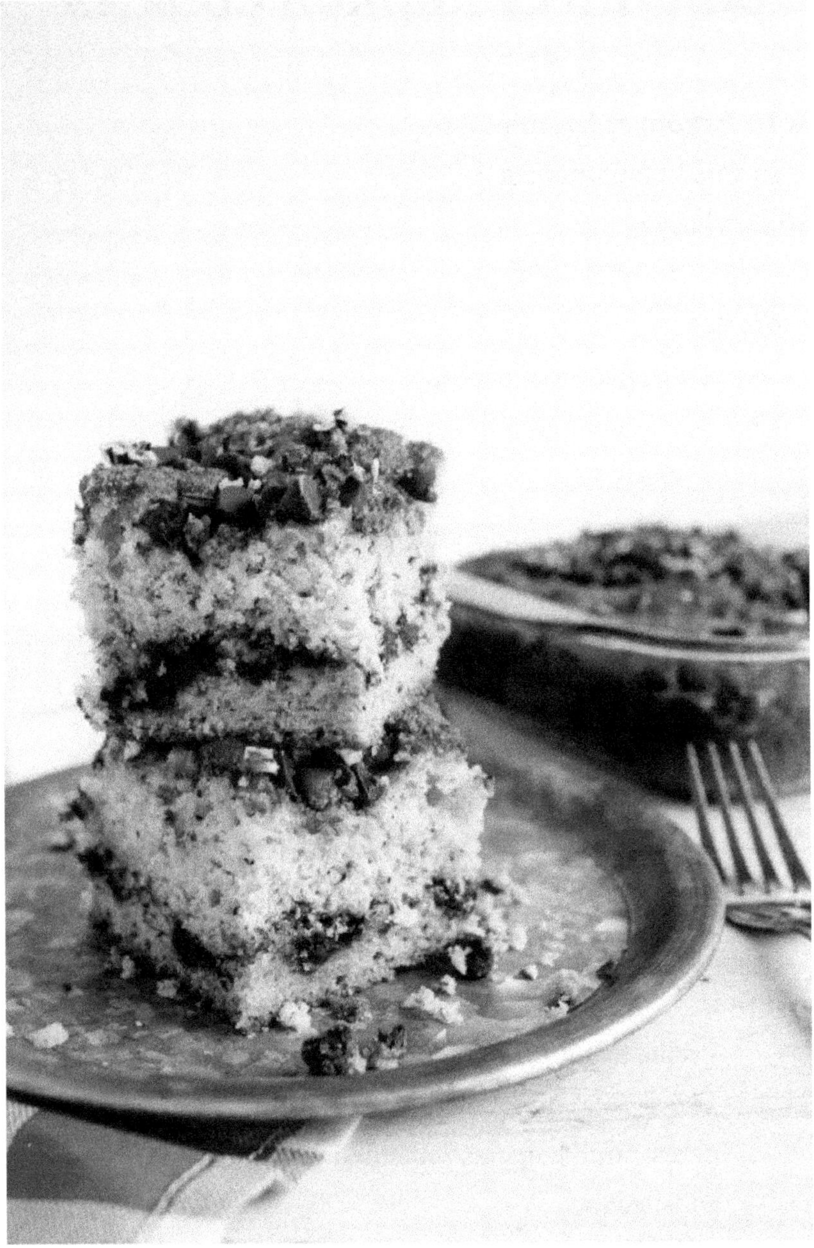

Banana Cinnamon Cookies

Time To Prepare: five minutes
Time to Cook: ten minutes
Yield: Servings 2

Ingredients:

- 2 ripe bananas, peeled
- ¼ cup almond milk, unsweetened
- 4 pitted dates
- 1 tablespoon cinnamon
- 1 teaspoon vanilla
- 1 ½ teaspoon lemon juice
- 3 tablespoons dried and chopped cranberries
- 1 teaspoon baking powder
- 2 tablespoons dried and chopped raisins
- 2/3 cup applesauce, unsweetened
- 2/3 cup coconut flour

Directions:

1. Preheat your oven to 350 degrees F.
2. Use a food processor to mix almond milk, applesauce, dates, and bananas. Blend until you achieve a smooth consistency.
3. Put in in coconut flour, baking powder, cinnamon, vanilla, and lemon juice. Blend for a minute. Fold in cranberries and raisins.

4. Pour a baking sheet with the cookie dough. Put inside the oven for about twenty minutes.

5. Let sit for five minutes and allow it to harden and serve.

Nutritional Info: ‖ Calories: 53 kcal ‖ Protein: 9.28 g ‖ Fat: 7.58 g ‖ Carbohydrates: 65.87 g

Beet Pancakes

Time To Prepare: ten minutes
Time to Cook: twelve minutes
Yield: Servings 3

Ingredients:

- ½ Cup Heavy Milk
- ½ Cup Melted Butter
- 1 Cup Flour
- 1 Large Egg
- 1 Tbsp. Baking Powder
- 1 Tsp. Vanilla Extract
- 1/3 Cup Plain Greek Yoghurt
- 1/4 Tsp Baking Soda
- 3 Cup Whole Wheat Flour
- 4 Cups Roasted Beet, Puree
- 6 Tsp. Brown Sugar
- Salt

Directions:

1. Combine the dry ingredients in a container.
2. In another container, combine the wet ingredients.
3. Mix both mixtures until the desired smoothness is achieved.
4. Fry the batter on a pan to make pancakes.

5. Serve with whip cream.

Nutritional Info: ‖ Calories: 359 kcal ‖ Carbohydrates: 60 g ‖ Fat: 3.0 g ‖ Protein: 18.4 g.

Berry Ice Pops

Time To Prepare: 3 Hours 5 Minutes
Time to Cook: 0 minutes
Yield: Servings 4

Ingredients:

- ¼ Cup Water
- 1 Cup Blueberries, Fresh or Frozen
- 1 Cup Strawberries, Fresh or Frozen
- 1 Teaspoon Lemon Juice, Fresh
- 2 Cups Whole Milk Yogurt, Plain
- 2 Tablespoons Honey, Raw

Directions:

1. Put all together the ingredients in a blender, and blend until the desired smoothness is achieved.
2. Pour into your molds, and freeze for minimum three hours before you serve.

Nutritional Info: ‖ Calories: 140 ‖ Protein: 5 Grams ‖ Fat: 4 Grams ‖ Carbohydrates: 23 Grams

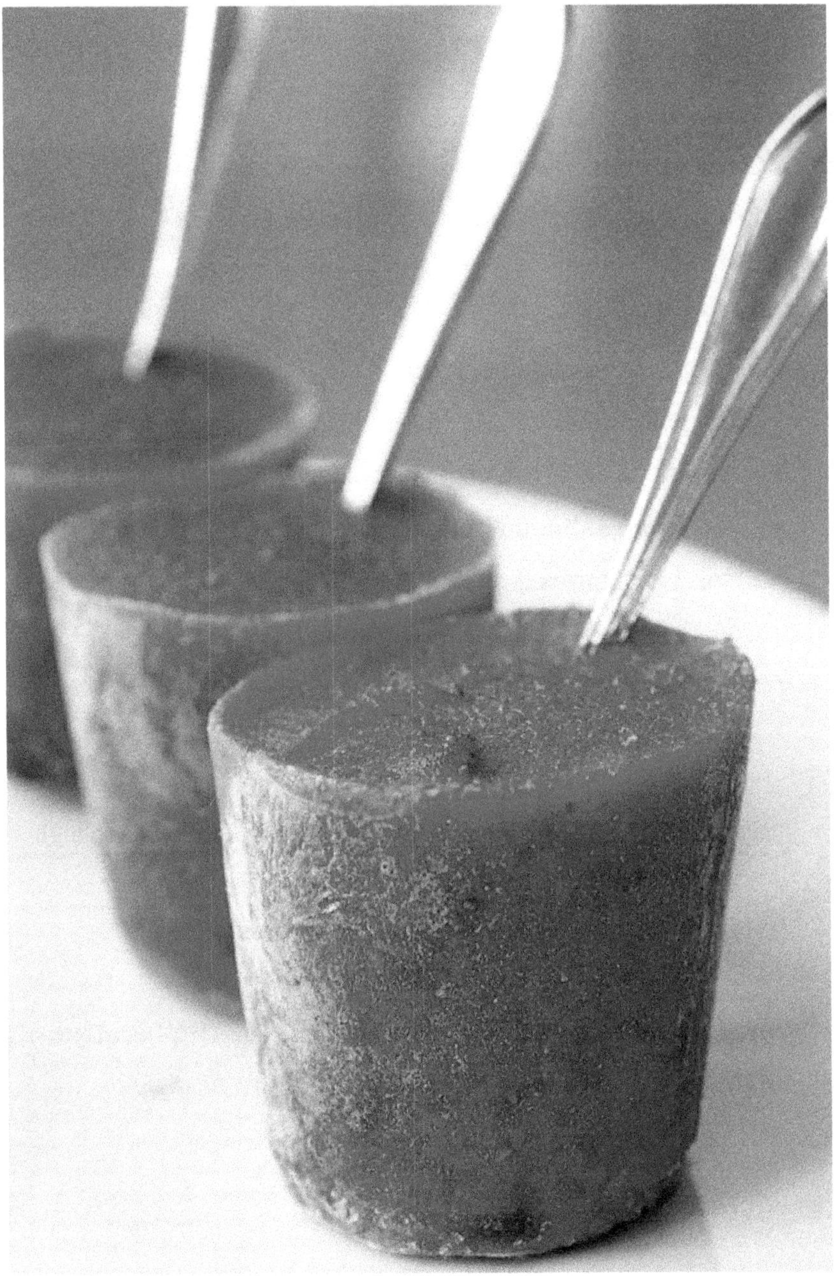

Berry Parfait

Time To Prepare: 10 min
Time to Cook: 10 min
Yield: Servings 5

Ingredients:

- 14oz / 400g mixed berries
- 2 tsp honey
- 3.5oz / 100g Greek yogurt
- 7oz / 200g almond butter
- 7oz / 200g mixed nuts

Directions:

1. Combine the Greek yogurt, butter, and honey until its smooth.
2. Put in a layer of berries and a layer of the mixture in a glass until it's full.
3. Serve instantly with sprinkled nuts.

Nutritional Info: ‖ Calories: 250 ‖ Carbohydrates: 17 g ‖ Protein: 7.2 g ‖ Fat: 19.4 g ‖ Sugar: 42.3 g ‖ Fiber: 6.6 g ‖ Sodium: 21 mg

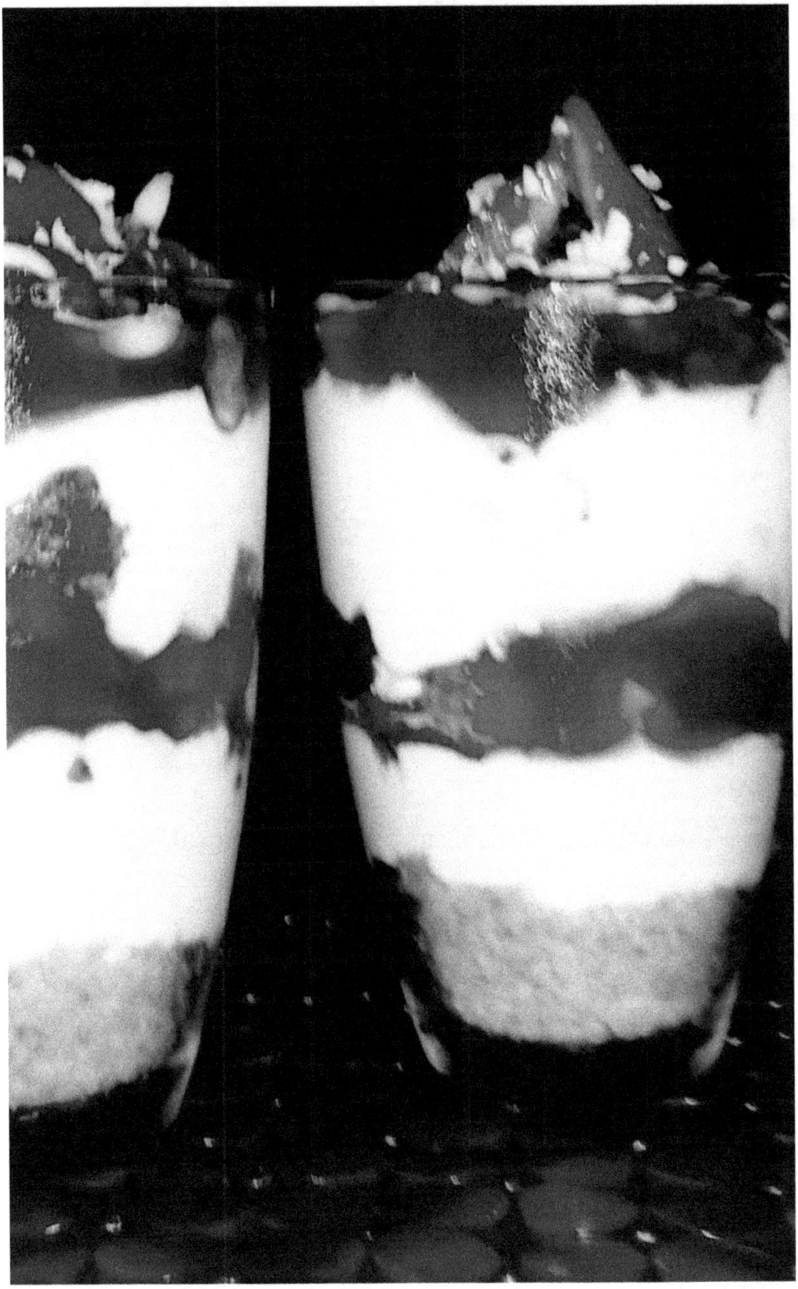

Berry-Banana Yogurt

Time To Prepare: ten minutes

Time to Cook: 0 minute

Yield: Servings 1

Ingredients:

- ¼ cup collard greens, chopped
- ¼ cup quick-cooking oats
- ½ banana, frozen fresh
- ½ cup blueberries, fresh and frozen
- 1 container 5.3ounes Greek yogurt, non-fat
- 1 cup almond milk
- 5-6 ice cubes

Directions:

1. Take microwave-safe cup and put in 1 cup almond milk and ¼ cup oats
2. Put the cups into your microwave on high for 2.5 minutes
3. When oats are cooked and 2 ice cubes to cool
4. Combine them well
5. Put in all ingredients in your blender

Blend until smooth and creamy

Best enjoyed chilled.

Nutritional Info: ‖ Calories: 379 ‖ Fat: 10g ‖ Carbohydrates: 63g ‖ Protein: 13g

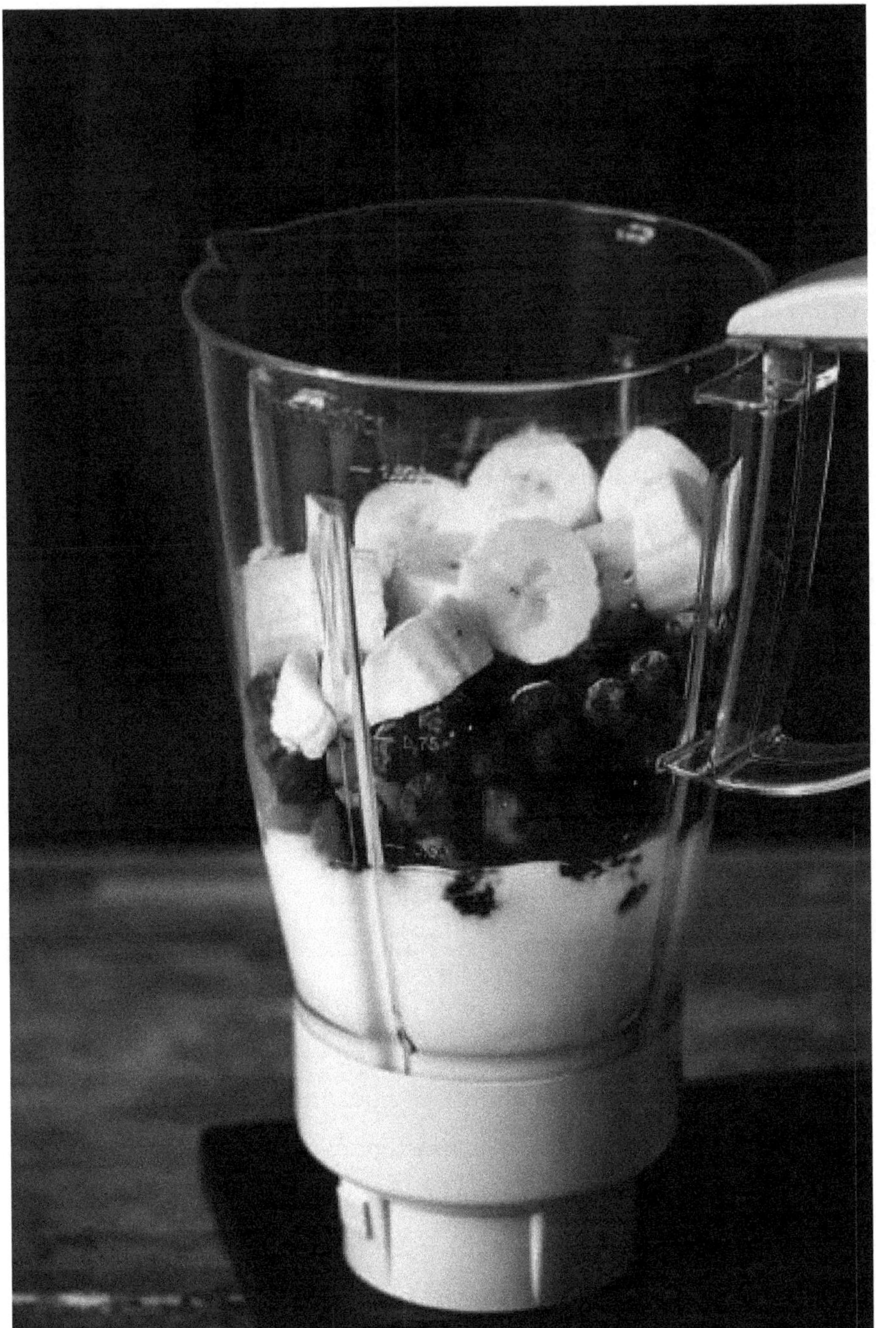

Black Tea Cake

Time To Prepare: ten minutes

Time to Cook: thirty-five minutes

Yield: Servings 10

Ingredients:

- ½ cup coconut butter
- ½ cup coconut oil
- 1 teaspoon baking soda
- 2 cups coconut milk
- 2 teaspoons vanilla extract
- 3 ½ cups almond flour
- 3 teaspoons baking powder
- 4 eggs
- 6 tablespoons black tea powder
- Chicory root powder to the taste

Directions:

1. Place the coconut milk in a pot and warm it up on moderate heat. Put in tea, stir thoroughly, take off the heat and cool down, In a container, mix the coconut butter with the chicory powder, eggs, vanilla, coconut oil, almond flour, baking soda, baking powder, and tea mix. Stir thoroughly, pour into a lined cake pan, and bake in your oven at 350 degrees F for half an hour Slice, split between plates, before you serve.

2. Enjoy!

Nutritional Info: ǁ Calories: 170 ǁ Fat: 4 ǁ Fiber: 5 ǁ Carbohydrates: 6 ǁ Protein: 2

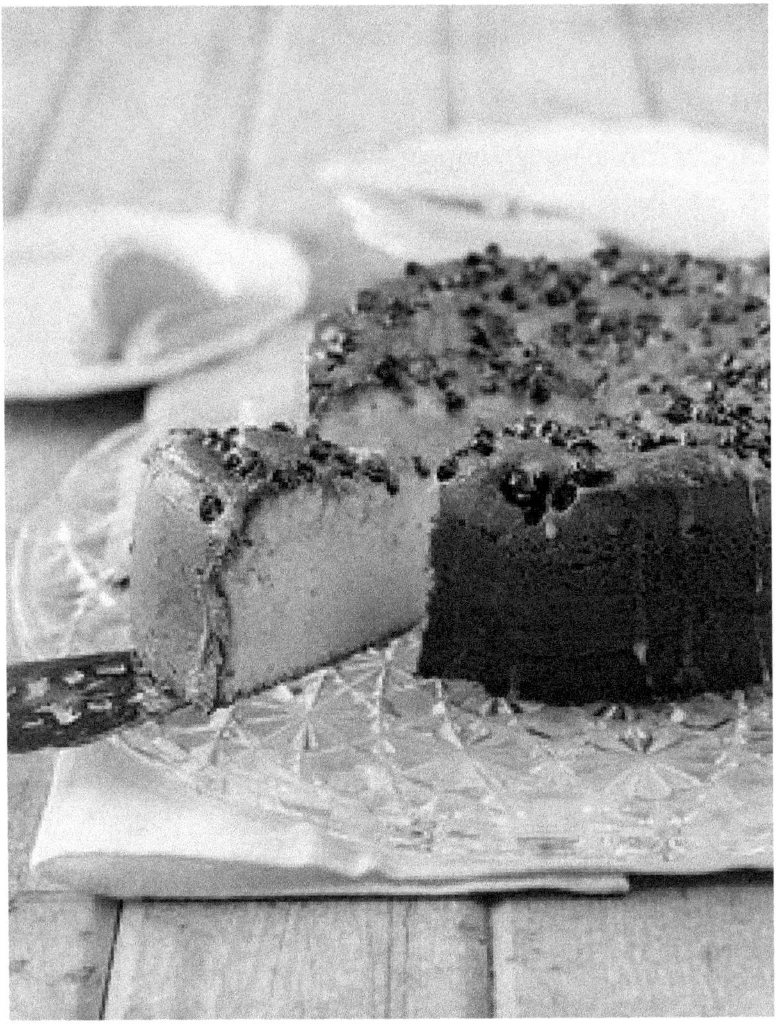

Blueberry Crisp

Time To Prepare: five minutes
Time to Cook: thirty minutes
Yield: Servings 4

Ingredients:

- ¼ cups pecans, chopped
- ¼ teaspoon nutmeg
- ½ teaspoon ginger
- 1 cup buckwheat
- 1 lb. blueberries
- 1 teaspoon of cinnamon
- 1 teaspoon of honey
- 2 tablespoons olive oil

Directions:

1. Preheat the oven to 350 degrees F.
2. Grease a baking dish.
3. Mix together the pecans, wheat, oil, spices, and honey in a container.
4. Put in the berries to your pan. Layer the topping on your berries.
5. Bake for thirty minutes at 350 F.

Nutritional Info: Calories 327 ‖ Carbohydrates: 35g ‖ Fat: 19g ‖ Protein: 4g ‖ Sugar: 14g ‖ Fiber: 5g ‖ Sodium: 2mg ‖ Potassium: 197mg

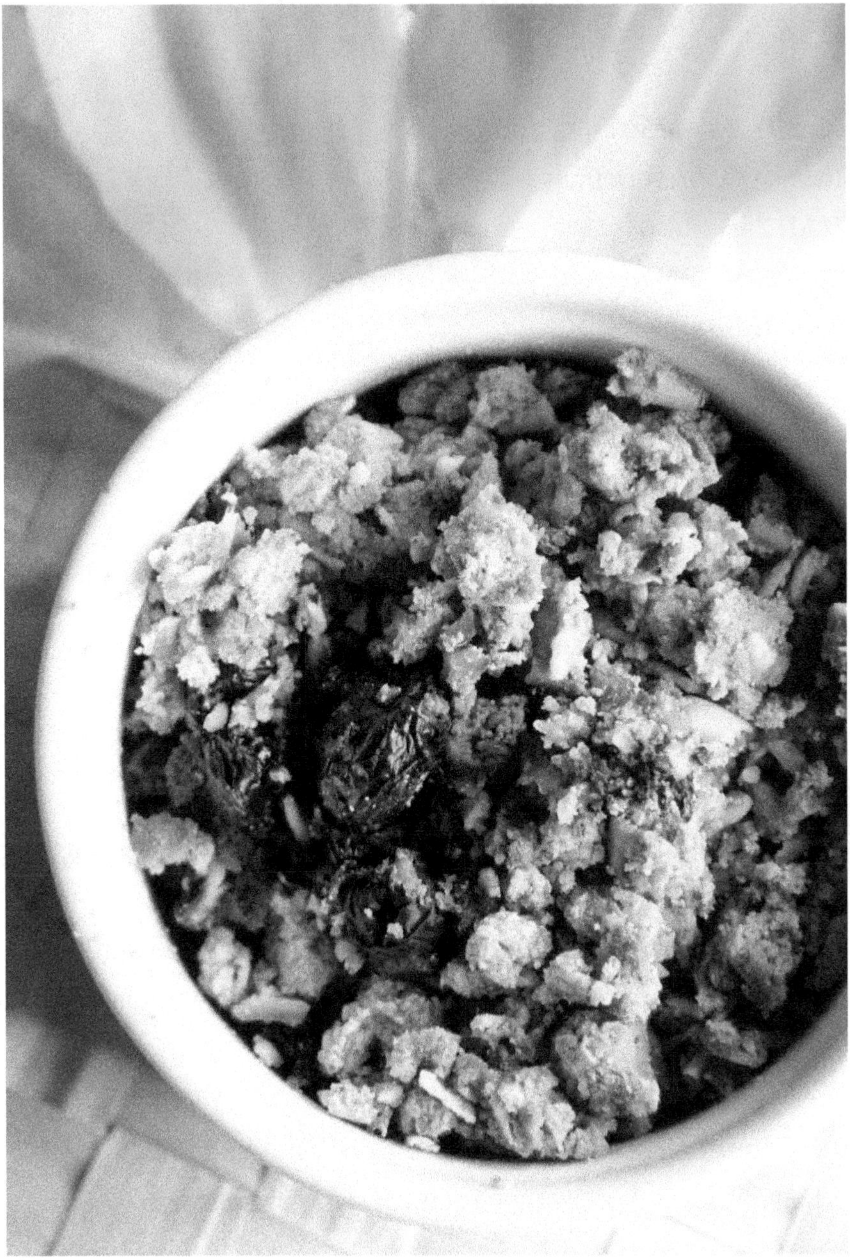

Blueberry Energy Bites

Time To Prepare: ten minutes
Time to Cook: 0 minutes
Yield: Servings 6

Ingredients:

- ¼ teaspoon of cinnamon
- ½ cup of gluten-free oat flour
- ½ cup of unsweetened almond milk
- ½ teaspoon of sea salt
- 2 tablespoons of dried blueberries
- 2 tablespoons of organic peanut butter
- 2 tablespoons of pure maple syrup

Directions:

1. Put the dry ingredients into a mixing container, including the peanut butter, and stir until blended.
2. Put in the almond milk and maple syrup, and stir.
3. Form into an inch balls, and place in your fridge to firm up before you serve.

Nutritional Info: ‖ Total Carbohydrates: 13g ‖ Fiber: 1g ‖ Net Carbohydrates: ‖ Protein: 3g ‖ Total Fat: 1g ‖ Calories: 93

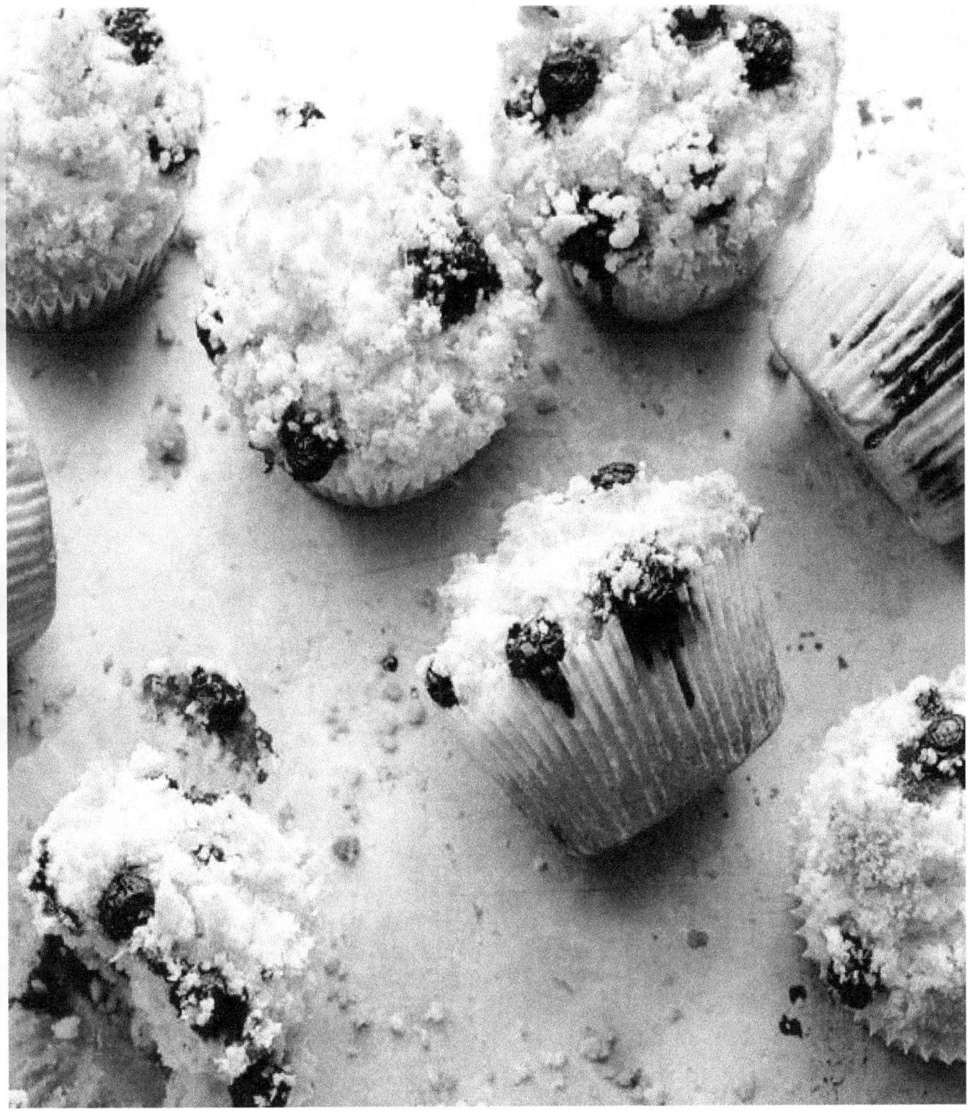

Blueberry Sour Cream Cake

Time To Prepare: twenty minutes

Time to Cook: 70 minutes

Yield: Servings 4

Ingredients:

- 1 Cup Blueberry
- 1 Cup Of Melted Butter
- 1 Cup Sour Cream
- 1 Tsp Vanilla Extract
- 1 Tsp. Baking Powder
- 1 Tsp. Cinnamon Powder
- 2 Cups Of Brown Sugar
- 2 Large Eggs
- 2 Tbsp. All-Purpose Flour
- Salt

Direction:

1. Preheat oven on 175C.
2. Mix together the butter and sugar till light and fluffy.
3. Put sour cream, vanilla extract, and eggs into the mixture.
4. In another container, put all together the dry ingredients then mix.
5. Place the dry mixture into the butter mixture, putting in blueberries, then mix well.

6. Put the batter into a greased pan then bake for about fifty minutes at 170C.
7. Serve with sour cream and blueberries.

Nutritional Info: ǁ Calories: 234 kcal ǁ Carbohydrates: 43 g ǁ Fat: 21 g ǁ Protein: 14.4 g.

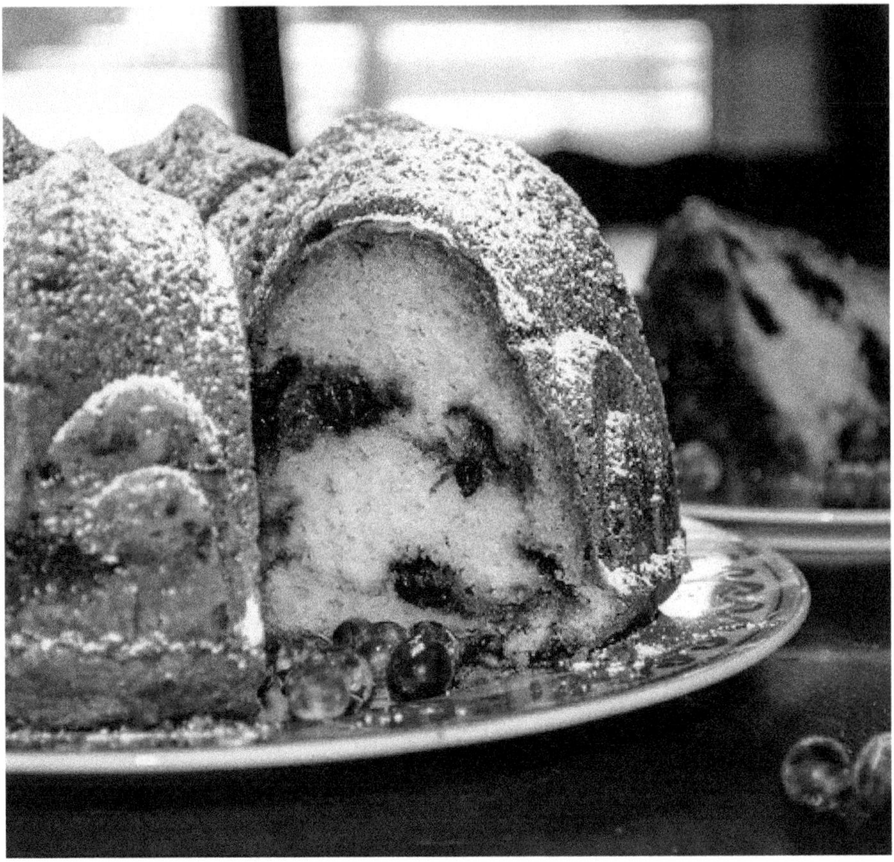

.

Lightning Source UK Ltd.
Milton Keynes UK
UKHW020647290621
386334UK00004B/22